Busy People's Low-Carb Cookbook

Dawn Hall

RUTLEDGE HILL PRESS
Nashville, Tennessee
A Division of Thomas Nelson Publishers
Since 1798

www.thomasnelson.com

It is with a grateful heart that I dedicate
this book to my three younger sisters, who I am
fortunate to have as friends also: Kellie Dashner,
Desireé Oberhouse, and Lana Leiniger.

(Okay, I said it. You are all younger than me. Now be kind
and don't rub salt in my wounds about my being the oldest
of all seven of us kids. Remember, it is not how old you are
but how old you feel that is most important.)

Copyright © 2005 by Dawn Hall

The authors and publisher of this book assume no liability for, and are released by readers from, any injury or damage resulting from the strict adherence to, or deviation from, the directions and/or recipes herein.

Rutledge Hill Press books may be purchased in bulk for educational, business, fundraising, or sales promotional use. For information, please e-mail SpecialMarkets@ThomasNelson.com.

Published by Rutledge Hill Press, a Division of Thomas Nelson, Inc., P.O. Box 141000, Nashville, Tennessee, 37214.

Library of Congress Cataloging-in-Publication Data

Hall, Dawn.
  Busy people's low-carb cookbook / Dawn Hall.
    p. cm.
  Includes index.
  ISBN 1-4016-0215-0 (hardcover)
  1. Low-carbohydrate diet—Recipes. 2. Quick and easy cookery. I. Title.
RM237.73.H345 2005
641.5'6383—dc22

2004028910

Printed in China

05 06 07 08 09—5 4 3 2 1

Complete Your Busy People's Library

The recipes in these cookbooks are all easy to prepare and cook. They all contain 7 ingredients or less and can be prepared in less than 30 minutes.

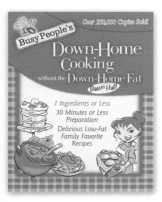

1-4016-0104-9
$16.99

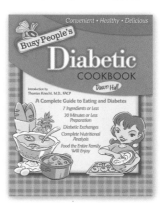

1-4016-0188-X
$16.99

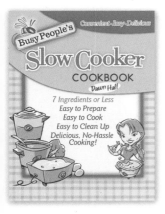

1-4016-0107-3
$16.99

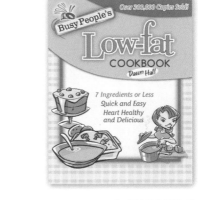

1-4016-0105-7
$16.99

RUTLEDGE HILL PRESS
Nashville, Tennessee
A Division of Thomas Nelson Publishers
Since 1798

www.thomasnelson.com

**Available at better book stores everywhere
or at www.RutledgeHillPress.com**

Contents

Special Thanks

Special thanks first and foremost to Larry Stone, founder and president of Rutledge Hill Press. I am so grateful for his belief in my abilities to produce a terrific low-carb cookbook.

Right in line with Larry, goes a special thanks to my literary agent, Coleen O'Shea. She, too, believed in my abilities and had faith that I could produce a top-quality, low-carb cookbook. Thus I did.

There are two other very special people I want to thank. This book could not have come about if it were not for their help: Karen Schwanbeck, kitchen assistant and friend, and Ashley Hall, my daughter and gifted recipe tester. There is no way I could have ever produced such delicious, quality dishes if it weren't for their help. It is not enough for me to just create recipes that fall within the nutritional guidelines of low-carb and low-fat. Each recipe I create has to taste absolutely delicious, or it doesn't make the book. That means many times one idea may need to be critiqued a few times before it is good enough to reach our high standards. Some recipes we could never get to taste good enough to be included in this cookbook, no matter how hard we tried. I take pride in knowing every single recipe has been taste tested and made in my very own home.

Tammi Hancock has been a lifesaver in producing the highest quality nutritional information and breakdowns for all of my cookbooks. I rely on her 100 percent and am extremely grateful to her for her precision detail and accuracy.

It would be unfair for me not to thank my loving husband, John Bialorucki, and my other beautiful daughter, Whitney Hall, for faithfully being my guinea pigs who taste-tested my numerous recipe creations every day. Often people think it'd be great to have something new or different to eat every night. But to be honest, it isn't all it's cracked up to be. So I thank my family, who diligently critiqued every recipe. Their feedback is priceless and is what helps me to continue creating award-winning recipes and cookbooks that keep helping others have healthier, easier lives.

I do want to personally take a moment to thank you, the customers, for making my Busy People's cookbooks one of the best-selling cookbook series around. I never would've dreamed back in 1994, when I self-published my first cookbook in order to raise money to pay for my husband's cancer treatments, that many years later these cookbooks would still be selling so strong. Thank you for telling your friends and family, and for helping spread the word about what a blessing Busy People's cookbooks have been in your life in helping you reach your weight-loss goals, lower your cholesterol, and feel happier and healthier than ever before.

Last, but surely not least, it is to God I give all the praise and glory for giving me the gift of creating recipes. I consider this gift every bit as much of an art as a painter creating a new painting or a songwriter writing a new song. So many of these unique and creative ideas were truly a gift from God. Often I even amaze myself at how well an idea will turn out. I know this cookbook is a "God Thing," and it is to Him I give all praise and glory.

Introduction

"Carbohydrate Overload"

Eating low-fat foods not only helps prevent cancer, heart disease, and diabetes, but according to Dr. Dean Ornish in his book *Eat More, Weigh Less,* it can even reverse heart disease. This is wonderful news for people like me, who have a history of heart disease and cancer on both sides of the family.

In the 1980s when low-fat became more prevalent, manufacturers jumped on the bandwagon, selling all kinds of low-fat and fat-free products. These processed products, however, were packed with simple carbohydrates known as sugars. Although the low-fat processed foods are better than the high-fat processed foods, they should still be eaten in moderation and only occasionally. Just because they are low in fat doesn't mean they aren't fattening. When you take in too many simple carbohydrates without extra exercise, they turn to fat. For good health, nothing compares to God's healthy foods, such as whole grains, fresh fruits, vegetables, and lean proteins.

Many people have the mind-set that fat-free is okay to eat till their heart's content without any concern to portion control. This kind of thinking has made Americans more overweight, out of shape, and feeling more fatigued than ever before. To top it off, people's hunger pangs kick into high gear, and they often feel more hungry shortly after they've eaten a bunch of processed, fat-free, compact, carbohydrate foods than if they'd eaten nothing at all.

It happened to me, too. Even though I was watching my diet, I was gaining weight. I joined the biblically-based, weight-loss support group First Place. I lost eight pounds of unhealthy, unwanted fat in twelve weeks and discovered that I had been on a "carbohydrate overload."

Simply put, I was eating too many processed simple carbohydrates that made me feel hungrier throughout the day.

I cut back on flour and sugar, and continued eating low-fat, healthy proteins along with all food groups such as fruits, vegetables, and whole grains. (Sorry folks, white flour, sugar, candy, and fried foods are not major food groups.)

I feel less hungry throughout the day, and my cravings have declined as well. Eating fewer carbohydrates, especially sugary foods, along with eating more fiber has helped me feel healthier and become leaner.

Many of us have heard of people's successful weight loss on the induction phase of Dr. Atkins' diet of eating mostly proteins and three cups of green vegetables daily. Regrettably, many people do not incorporate healthy fruits, vegetables, and whole grains in appropriate serving sizes as the doctor had intended. Another down side is that the healthier, lower-fat proteins are often not selected by dieters.

We have figured out that it's not just the simple carbohydrates that we need to worry about; we also need to watch our fat. At first I was skeptical about the low-carb craze because it seemed like the diets were too high in fat. But after doing some research, I found that low-carb diets can be low-fat, too, just without all the sugars that come from simple carbohydrates.

There are some staple products that have been made healthier thanks to the low-carbohydrate, high-fiber awareness. Some excellent examples are the low-carbohydrate flour tortillas, pastas, and breads, which all have much more fiber. Unfortunately, the higher the consumer demand, the higher the cost tends to be as well. This proves to be the case now with low-carbohydrate, high-fiber foods also. Hopefully these products will be more budget friendly in the near future. However, for the time being, when we see low-carb, higher-fiber tortillas, pastas, and breads on sale, we are going to have to stock up on them in order to save on cost in the long run. When looking for low-carb and low-fat foods, beware of the serving sizes. Sometimes manufacturers will cut the serving size in half, or more, what a normal person eats in order to get away with calling it low-carb or low-fat. It's a shame, but it's a fact.

You may have gotten on the low-carb bandwagon long before I did, but now I want to give you some great low-carb recipes to make it easier for you. I hope you enjoy my recipes in this book that deliciously unite the two healthy diets: low-fat and low-carb. By the way, for those people who think they don't like low-fat foods and only want to do the low-carb diet, please don't tell them that these recipes are both low-carb and low-fat. Just let them love eating my recipes. I figure some things are better left unsaid. Enjoy!

Refreshing Refreshments

Sweet & Sour Lemon-Berry Freeze

Kids who like sour things especially get a kick out of this treat because the tart flavor reminds them of sweet tart candy.

1¹/₄ cups blueberries	1 cup ice
2 cups sugar-free lemonade	¹/₂ cup Splenda Granular, measures like sugar

- Put the blueberries, lemonade, ice, and Splenda in a blender.
- Cover and process on the highest speed for 1 to 2 minutes or until smooth.

Yield: 4 (1-cup) servings

Calories: 40 (0% fat); Total Fat: 0 gm; Cholesterol: 0 mg; Carbohydrate: 10 gm;
Dietary Fiber: 1 gm; Protein: 0 gm; Sodium: 1 mg
Diabetic Exchanges: ¹/₂ fruit

Preparation Time: 3 minutes or less

Menu Idea: This is so super thick that it makes a great midday snack on a hot day.

Virgin Frozen Strawberry Daiquiri

I was elated at how wonderfully delicious, smooth, fruity, and refreshing this turned out. I'm equally as thrilled at how much money I will be able to save making them at home for a fraction of the cost then in restaurants.

8 ounces no-sugar-added frozen strawberries	1 tablespoon fat-free dessert whipped topping
1½ cups sugar-free lemonade	10 to 12 individual packets Splenda

- Put the strawberries, lemonade, dessert topping, and Splenda in a blender.
- Cover and process on the highest speed for 1 to 2 minutes or until smooth and creamy.
- Serve immediately in pretty glasses.

Note: For a fancier presentation, dip the rim of the glass in a plate of water. Then dip the wet rimmed glass into the Splenda. The Splenda will cling to the rim of the glass.

Yield: 2½ (1-cup) servings

Calories: 57 (0% fat); Total Fat: 0 gm; Cholesterol: 0 mg; Carbohydrate: 14 gm; Dietary Fiber: 2 gm; Protein: 0 gm; Sodium: 9 mg
Diabetic Exchanges: 1 fruit

Preparation time: 3 minutes or less

Menu Idea: Great for special dinners or luncheons. Because the primary ingredients are strawberries, I consider this a fruit serving for the day as well. I really can't think of a meal with which this wouldn't taste good.

Tropical Fruit Breeze

This is a great frozen drink to serve for Hawaiian-themed parties. Children also feel pretty special when served this special treat. For extra-added fun, serve this to children in little plastic, fruit-shaped beverage containers.

1	cup sugar-free orange drink	1/2	teaspoon imitation banana flavoring
1	cup ice (about 7 ice cubes)	2	tablespoons crushed pineapple

- Put the orange drink, ice, banana flavoring, and crushed pineapple in a blender.
- Cover and process on the highest speed for 1 minute, or until all the ice is crushed and the beverage is smooth.

Yield: 2½ (1-cup) servings

Calories: 11 (0% fat); Total Fat: 0 gm; Cholesterol: 0 mg; Carbohydrate: 2 gm;
Dietary Fiber: 0 gm; Protein: 0 gm; Sodium: 1 mg
Diabetic Exchanges: Free

 Preparation time: 3 minutes or less

Menu Idea: For a Hawaiian-themed luncheon, serve this along with Hawaiian Chicken Spread (with only 3 carbs) on page 108 and Coconut Sugar Cookies (with 6 carbs) on page 233, both in *Busy People's Diabetic Cookbook*. Oh, and don't forget a fresh fruit tray too. The Strawberry Fruit Dip on page 83 in this cookbook will go perfectly with it.

Peachy-Keen Smoothie

It's so wonderful having delicious and healthy alternatives in place of those high-calorie, unhealthy, and overpriced smoothies at ice cream parlors. You'll probably never miss carbohydrate-loaded smoothies again after you've enjoyed this.

2 cups no-sugar-added frozen peaches, not thawed	1/2 cup ice cubes (about 4 ice cubes)
1 1/2 cups sugar-free, peach-flavored sparkling water	1 to 2 individual packets Splenda (optional)
1/2 cup no-sugar-added, fat-free frozen vanilla yogurt	

- In a blender put the peaches, sparkling water, frozen yogurt, and ice cubes.
- Put the lid of the blender on, and process for about 2 minutes or until smooth and creamy.
- If desired, add the Splenda, one packet at a time.

Yield: 3 (1-cup) servings

Calories: 87 (10% fat); Total Fat: 1 gm; Cholesterol: 1 mg; Carbohydrate: 17 gm; Dietary Fiber: 3 gm; Protein: 2 gm; Sodium: 30 mg
Diabetic Exchanges: 1 fruit

Preparation time: 3 minutes or less

Menu Idea: This is very refreshing as a midday snack on a hot day. Try it with Stuffed Celery Sticks on page 73 of this book for something a little crunchy that'll be good added protein when eaten with this smoothie.

Frozen Fuzzy Orange Smoothie

The title sounds like an oxymoron, doesn't it? How can a drink be fuzzy and a smoothie in the same drink? Believe me — you'll really enjoy this delightful flavor combination of peaches and oranges blended together. I created this drink using sugar-free orange drink instead of real mandarin oranges to cut down on the carbs. I'm quite pleased with the results.

3 cups no-sugar-added frozen peaches, not thawed	8 individual packets Splenda
2 cups sugar-free orange drink	

- Put the peaches, orange drink, and Splenda in a blender.
- Put the lid on and process for about 2 minutes or until smooth and slushy.

Yield: 3½ (1-cup) servings

Calories: 81 (11% fat); Total Fat: 1 gm; Cholesterol: 0 mg; Carbohydrate: 16 gm; Dietary Fiber: 3 gm; Protein: 1 gm; Sodium: 0 mg
Diabetic Exchanges: 1 fruit

Preparation time: 5 minutes or less

Menu Idea: This is a marvelous drink for those days you crave something sweet, but you don't want to blow eating healthy. I like to use this drink as my way of getting my fruit for the day. Often I'll serve it at picnics, cookouts, or in the middle of the afternoon for a midday snack.

Shock Tart Smoothie

Kids (young and old alike) who like sweet tarts will love this specialty drink. The first time I tasted this fun smoothie, it definitely made my taste buds soar.

6	cups ice cubes (about 42 ice cubes)	3	teaspoons sugar-free lemonade mix (do not make as directed)
1/2	cup fat-free, low-carb milk	1	cup cold water
1	(8-ounce) container fat-free, frozen dessert whipped topping		

- Put the ice, milk, whipped topping, lemonade mix, and water in a blender.
- Cover and process on high for 2 minutes or until smooth. All the ice should be crushed.
- Spoon into dessert cups and eat right away.

Yield: 5½ (1-cup) servings

Calories: 76 (0% fat); Total Fat: 0 gm; Cholesterol: 0 mg; Carbohydrate: 14 gm; Dietary Fiber: 0 gm; Protein: 1 gm; Sodium: 42 mg
Diabetic Exchanges: 1 other carbohydrate

Preparation time: 5 minutes or less

Menu Idea: This is fun to eat on a hot day with fresh, crunchy vegetables, such as sliced cucumbers and red or yellow bell peppers straight from the garden or farmers' market.

Triple-Thick Strawberry Cream Smoothie

This super-thick smoothie is almost like soft-served strawberry ice cream. It's dense enough for you to eat it with a spoon, or you can drink it with a straw if you have a lot of suction power. Because it is such a good source of low-calorie carbohydrates and nonfat protein, this also makes a good meal replacement. I especially like having two servings (equaling 16 ounces total) in place of a light breakfast or lunch. As a dessert, put each serving into a dessert cup, and top with a fresh strawberry.

1¹/₂ cups fat-free, low-carb milk	1 teaspoon vanilla extract
1 (16-ounce) bag no-sugar-added frozen strawberries, not thawed	¹/₂ cup Splenda Granular, measures like sugar

- Put the milk, strawberries, vanilla, and Splenda in a blender.
- Cover and process on the highest speed for 1 to 2 minutes or until smooth and creamy. You may need to turn the blender off occasionally and press the frozen strawberries into the blender.

Yield: 4 (1-cup) servings

Calories: 81 (0% fat); Total Fat: 0 gm; Cholesterol: 2 mg; Carbohydrate: 15 gm; Dietary Fiber: 2 gm; Protein: 5 gm; Sodium: 81 mg
Diabetic Exchanges: 1 fruit, 1 very lean meat

Preparation time: 3 minutes or less

Menu Idea: Eat this with a spoon for a refreshing and nutritious afternoon snack.

Cherry Chocolate Chip Smoothie

This is just what the doctor ordered to curb your sweet tooth, whether for a midday or late afternoon snack. It is low in calories and carbohydrates, yet has enough protein to not drive your blood sugar through the roof and get your cravings riled-up like a lot of regular smoothies.

1 cup fat-free, low-carb milk	¹/₂ teaspoon sugar-free cherry
1 cup ice (about 7 ice cubes)	drink mix (do not make as
1 cup no-sugar-added, reduced-fat	directed)
chocolate chip cherry ice cream	

- Put the milk, ice, ice cream, and drink mix in a blender.
- Cover and process on high for about 1 minute or until smooth and creamy. There will be little chunks of chocolate; however, the ice should be all crushed and smooth.

Yield: 3 (1-cup) servings

Calories: 81 (0% fat); Total Fat: 0 gm; Cholesterol: 2 mg; Carbohydrate: 14 gm; Dietary Fiber: 0 gm; Protein: 6 gm; Sodium: 105 mg
Diabetic Exchanges: ¹/₂ skim milk, ¹/₂ other carbohydrate

 Preparation time: 3 minutes or less

 Menu Idea: This smoothie makes a fine snack all by itself. However, if you feel like you need more protein, then have a piece of turkey breast lunchmeat rolled up on the side.

Coconut Cream Smoothie

This terrific smoothie makes a wonderful breakfast-on-the-run, especially on mornings when the weather is hot.

2 cups fat-free, low-carb milk	1 cup fat-free dessert whipped topping
2 cups ice (about 14 ice cubes)	
1 teaspoon coconut imitation flavoring (found near vanilla extract)	3 tablespoons Splenda Granular, measures like sugar
1/2 teaspoon vanilla extract	1/2 tablespoon shredded coconut

- Put the milk, ice, coconut flavoring, vanilla, whipped topping, Splenda, and coconut in a blender.
- Cover and process on the highest speed for about 3 minutes or until smooth and creamy. You may have to turn the blender off occasionally and press the ice cubes down to ensure there are no chunks of ice remaining.

Yield: 5 (1-cup) servings

Calories: 62 (0% fat); Total Fat: 0 gm; Cholesterol: 2 mg; Carbohydrate: 7 gm; Dietary Fiber: 0 gm; Protein: 5 gm; Sodium: 94 mg
Diabetic Exchanges: 1/2 skim milk

Preparation time: 3 minutes or less

Menu Idea: If you want a little extra protein, just eat a slice of lunchmeat or a hard-boiled egg along with it. However, I find two servings (sixteen ounces total) of this for breakfast satisfying and filling enough.

Extra-Thick Peach Milkshake

Even though this recipe doesn't have a lot of milk in it, it tastes like a milkshake because of the dessert topping and vanilla extract. This is smooth, creamy, and delicious with just the right amount of sweet and tangy flavor we peach lovers love.

2 cups frozen peaches, still frozen, not thawed	1/4 teaspoon vanilla extract
1/2 cup fat-free, frozen dessert whipped topping	3/4 cup sugar-free orange flavored drink, chilled
1/2 cup fat-free, low-carb milk	1/4 cup Splenda Granular, measures like sugar*

- Put the peaches, frozen topping, milk, vanilla, orange drink, and Splenda in a blender.
- Process on the highest speed for 1 to 2 minutes or until smooth. You may have to turn the blender off and on occasionally to press the frozen ingredients to the bottom.
- Serve immediately.

Note: Taste before serving. Add more Splenda, 1 teaspoon at a time, if needed until desired sweetness is achieved. Peaches vary in degrees of sweetness, so the amount of sweetener will vary.

Yield: 2 (1-cup) servings

Calories: 143 (7% fat); Total Fat: 1 gm; Cholesterol: 1 mg; Carbohydrate: 26 gm; Dietary Fiber: 4 gm; Protein: 4 gm; Sodium: 63 mg
Diabetic Exchanges: 1 fruit, 1/2 other carbohydrate, 1/2 very lean meat

 **Preparation time:** 3 minutes or less

Menu Idea: So thick and satisfying, I like this as a light breakfast on a hot day.

Banana-Blueberry Milkshake

You are probably wondering, "How in the world can she make a banana milkshake low in carbs when bananas are loaded with concentrated carbs?" Well here's my little secret: I use imitation banana flavoring found in the baking aisle near the vanilla extract.

1 cup blueberries (fresh or frozen)	1/2 teaspoon imitation banana flavoring
3 to 4 tablespoons Splenda Granular, measures like sugar	1 cup ice cubes (about 7 ice cubes)
1 cup fat-free, low-carb milk	
1 cup fat-free, no-sugar-added frozen vanilla yogurt	

- Put the blueberries, Splenda, milk, frozen yogurt, banana flavoring, and ice cubes into a blender.
- Put the lid on the blender. Turn the blender on highest speed for about 30 seconds to 1 minute or until smooth.
- Pour into glasses.

Yield: 3½ (1-cup) servings

Calories: 107 (5% fat); Total Fat: 1 gm; Cholesterol: 4 mg; Carbohydrate: 19 gm; Dietary Fiber: 2 gm; Protein: 6 gm; Sodium: 104 mg
Diabetic Exchanges: ½ fruit, 1 other carbohydrate, 1 very lean meat

 **Preparation time:** 3 minutes or less

Menu Idea: Because this is so healthy I'll have it for a breakfast on the run. I'm sure body builders could add their protein mix to this as well. This is also super with a light lunch such as Popeye's Favorite Salad (spinach salad, of course, with only 4 carbs), on page 143, in *Busy People's Diabetic Cookbook.*

Raspberry Milkshake

Oh, man! This is so delicious and refreshing. I love it. Without a doubt, you can tell by tasting the tiny seeds that this is no run-of-the-mill, generic, raspberry milkshake. Expect request for seconds. If you are like me, you'll be disappointed when your last sip is gone. It is that good.

1 cup fat-free, no-sugar-added frozen vanilla yogurt	2 tablespoons Splenda Granular, measures like sugar*
1 cup ice (about 7 ice cubes)	1/4 teaspoon sugar-free raspberry drink mix
1 cup fat-free, low-carb milk	
1/3 cup fresh raspberries, washed	

- Put the frozen yogurt, ice cubes, milk, raspberries, Splenda, and raspberry drink mix in a blender.
- Cover. Turn the blender to highest speed for about 30 seconds to 1 minute or until smooth.
- Pour into glasses.

Note: Add more Splenda if needed, 1 teaspoon at a time.

Yield: 3½ (1-cup) servings

Calories: 87 (5% fat); Total Fat: 1 gm; Cholesterol: 4 mg; Carbohydrate: 14 gm; Dietary Fiber: 2 gm; Protein: 6 gm; Sodium: 104 mg
Diabetic Exchanges: 1 other carbohydrate, 1 very lean meat

Preparation time: 3 minutes or less

Menu Idea: I actually shared this with a friend, and drank 1½ servings as a light lunch for a great low-carb and healthy-protein combination. For an easy low-carb cookout (using recipes all from this book), serve this along with Grilled and Lightly Barbequed Shrimp Kebabs on page 168, Sesame Seed Coleslaw on page 126, and Bacon, Lettuce, and Tomato Slices on page 114.

Three Berries Slushy

Here's a refreshing drink that's also a terrific way to get your daily requirement of fruit.

4	cups frozen mixed berries (raspberries, blueberries, and blackberries), not thawed	2	individual packets Splenda
		$1/3$	cup cold water
I	cup sugar-free lemon-lime soda		

- Put frozen berries, soda, Splenda, and water in a blender.
- Cover and process on the highest speed for 1 to 2 minutes or until smooth.
- Serve in glasses.

Yield: $2\frac{1}{2}$ (1-cup) servings

Calories: 131 (0% fat); Total Fat: 0 gm; Cholesterol: 0 mg; Carbohydrate: 33 gm; Dietary Fiber: 8 gm; Protein: 2 gm; Sodium: 14 mg
Diabetic Exchanges: 2 fruit

Preparation time: 3 minutes or less

Menu Idea: This is a terrific treat on a hot day.

Watermelon Slushy

Here's a creative way to use watermelon that kids just love.

4	plus 2 cups frozen watermelon*, not thawed	$^1/_2$	cup Splenda Granular, measures like sugar
I	cup cold water	I	tablespoon lime juice

- In a blender put the 4 cups watermelon, water, Splenda, and lime juice. Cover and process on highest speed for about 1 minute.
- Add the remaining 2 cups watermelon. Cover and process on highest speed for another minute or two until smooth.
- Pour into glasses.

Note: Cut the watermelon into pieces and freeze it in Ziploc bags. When ready to make the slushy, let the watermelon sit to slightly thaw about 10 minutes to soften in order to put the watermelon into a measuring cup.

Yield: 5½ (1-cup) servings

Calories: 59 (0% fat); Total Fat: 0 gm; Cholesterol: 0 mg; Carbohydrate: 15 gm; Dietary Fiber: 1 gm; Protein: 1 gm; Sodium: 2 mg
Diabetic Exchanges: 1 fruit

Preparation time: 15 minutes or less (including watermelons slightly thawing to soften)

Menu Idea: This is terrific with the Weenie Wraps with Cheese on page 64 in this book and fresh green, red, and yellow bell pepper sticks to dip into the Sweet & Sour Bacon Salad Dressing (with only 3 carbs) on page 62 in *Busy People's Down-Home Cooking Without the Down-Home Fat.*

Caribbean Lemonade Slushy

This is so refreshing. It's hard to believe it is low-carb. If you don't tell anyone it's low-carb, they'd never know by tasting it.

2	cups ice cubes (about 14 ice cubes)	1	cup fat-free, sugar-free, frozen vanilla yogurt
2	cups sugar-free lemonade	3/4	cup diet lemon-lime soda
1/2	teaspoon sugar-free lemonade drink mix (do not make as directed)		

- Put the ice cubes, lemonade, lemonade drink mix, frozen yogurt, and soda in a blender.
- Cover and process on highest speed for 1 to 2 minutes or until smooth and slushy.

Yield: 4½ (1-cup) servings

Calories: 50 (0% fat); Total Fat: 0 gm; Cholesterol: 2 mg; Carbohydrate: 9 gm; Dietary Fiber: 1 gm; Protein: 2 gm; Sodium: 44 mg
Diabetic Exchanges: ½ other carbohydrate

Preparation time: 3 minutes or less

Menu Idea: I like drinking this on a hot day because it's just the right blend of sweet and sour. It's great for swim parties, cookouts, and barbeques as well. For terrific entrée ideas look at the many recipes available in *Busy People's Down-Home Cooking Without the Down-Home Fat.* Some of my favorite recipes for these types of parties are the Pigs on a Stick on page 121 and Steak on a Stick (with only 1 little carb) on page 120 in that cookbook.

Blueberry Blitz Slushy

This is so good that I have a difficult time not drinking all of it at once.

2$\frac{1}{2}$ cups diet lemon-lime soda	$\frac{1}{4}$ cup Splenda Granular, measures like sugar
2 cups frozen blueberries, not thawed	1 ($\frac{1}{4}$-ounce) envelope unflavored gelatin (do not make as directed)*
2 cups ice cubes (about 14 ice cubes)	
$\frac{1}{4}$ teaspoon almond extract	

- In a blender put the soda, blueberries, ice, almond extract, Splenda, and gelatin, and process on highest speed for 1 to 2 minutes or until smooth.

Note: There are 4 envelopes in a 1-ounce box.

Yield: 5$\frac{1}{2}$ (1-cup) servings

Calories: 38 (0% fat); Total Fat: 0 gm; Cholesterol: 0 mg; Carbohydrate: 8 gm; Dietary Fiber: 2 gm; Protein: 1 gm; Sodium: 19 mg
Diabetic Exchanges: $\frac{1}{2}$ fruit

Preparation time: 5 minutes or less

Menu Idea: This is great with fat-free hot dogs, or for an afternoon pick-me-up snack.

Punch Bowl Raspberry Spritzer

This beautiful punch makes a lovely centerpiece for showers or ladies' teas or special occasion buffets such as Easter. Simply set the punchbowl with pretty glasses in the center of the table, and arrange the food, starting at the centerpiece and working your way outward.

1 (2-liter) bottle diet lemon-lime-flavored soda, chilled	2 quarts sugar-free raspberry drink mix (make as directed—I use Kool-Aid)
24 frozen raspberries	
1 lemon, cut into 8 slices	3 sprigs fresh mint (optional)

- Put the soda, raspberries, lemon slices, and Kool-Aid in a punch bowl. The fruit will float to the top and look really pretty.
- Place the sprigs of mint on top to garnish.

Note: For a fancier presentation, freeze 2 cups of the lemon-lime soda in a Bundt pan (about 2 hours). To release the frozen soda place the bottom of the pan in some hot water. Then place the frozen soda mold into the punch bowl with the fruit and garnish.

Yield: 16 (1-cup) servings

Calories: 4 (0% fat); Total Fat: 0 gm; Cholesterol: 0 mg; Carbohydrate: 0 gm; Dietary Fiber: 0 gm; Protein: 0 gm; Sodium: 19 mg
Diabetic Exchanges: Free

Preparation time: 5 minutes or less

Menu Idea: For a pretty dessert buffet, set this punch bowl in the center of an array of assorted low-carb cookies, such as the ones found in *Busy People's Low-Fat Cookbook:* Apple Spice Cookies (with only 5 carbs) on page 220 and Carrot Cookies (with only 6 carbs) on page 222.

Lemon-Lime Spritzer

This recipe makes thirteen very impressive and pretty drinks; however, you can make only a few at a time.

2 quarts sugar-free lemonade (make as directed)	78 ice cubes (6 per glass)
6 cups diet lemon-lime soda	2 lemons, cut into a total of 13 thin slices
½ cup Splenda Granular	3 limes, cut into a total of 13 thin slices
½ cup water	

- In a gallon jug stir together the lemonade and soda until well blended.
- Put the Splenda in a shallow bowl. Dip the rim of a tall glass into water about ¼-inch deep and then into the Splenda. Turn the glass a quarter turn to help the Splenda attach to the rim of the glass.
- Into the glass layer 2 ice cubes, 1 lemon slice, 2 more ice cubes, 1 lime slice, and 2 more ice cubes on top of the lime slice.
- Pour 1 cup of the lemon-lime spritzer over the ice. Serve immediately.
- Repeat the steps for the remaining servings.

Yield: 13 (8-ounce) servings

Calories: 7 (0% fat); Total Fat: 0 gm; Cholesterol: 0 mg; Carbohydrate: 1 gm; Dietary Fiber: 0 gm; Protein: 0 gm; Sodium: 16 mg
Diabetic Exchanges: Free

⏱ **Preparation time:** 10 minutes or less

🍴 **Menu Idea:** These are great for a cookout on a hot day. At our cookout I served a Marinated Grilled Chicken Breast (with only 2 carbs) on page 105 along with the Portobello Garlic Mushrooms on page 13, both in *Busy People's Down-Home Cooking Without the Down-Home Fat.*

Tomato Juice Cooler

This flavor combination kept coming to my thoughts sporadically for days. So I finally gave in, and I created this beverage for breakfast one morning. It was much smoother and more refreshing than I had anticipated it'd be. I really like it, and I know you will, too.

1/2 cup sugar-free lemonade, chilled	Pinch of celery salt
1/2 cup reduced-sodium tomato juice, chilled	1 lemon wedge or small stalk celery (optional)

- In a cup stir the lemonade, tomato juice, and celery salt together until well blended.
- Serve in a pretty glass. If desired, garnish with the lemon wedge or small celery stalk.

Yield: 1 (1-cup) serving

Calories: 32 (0% fat); Total Fat: 0 gm; Cholesterol: 0 mg; Carbohydrate: 7 gm; Dietary Fiber: 0 gm; Protein: 1 gm; Sodium: 152 mg
Diabetic Exchanges: 1$\frac{1}{2}$ vegetable

Preparation time: 2 minutes or less

Menu Idea: This is especially great for breakfast or brunch with egg-based entrées such as Mushroom & Onion Frittata (with 12 carbs) on page 91 in *Busy People's Down-Home Cooking Without the Down-Home Fat* or Spinach Scramble (with only 5 carbs) on page 68 in *Busy People's Diabetic Cookbook.*

Tomato Juice Cocktail

Replace serving the traditional high-carbohydrate and compact-calorie cup of orange juice with this delightful beverage for breakfast or brunch. You'll be glad you did. You'll never miss orange juice again. The slight sweetness cuts down on the acid of this refreshing cocktail.

2 cups tomato juice	1 individual packet Splenda
¼ teaspoon Worcestershire sauce	2 small, clean stems celery with leaves still on (optional)
¼ teaspoon Tabasco	
¼ teaspoon Mrs. Dash minced onion medley seasoning (found in the spice aisle)	

- Stir tomato juice, Worcestershire sauce, Tabasco, onion medley seasoning, and Splenda together until well blended.
- Pour into individual fancy juice glasses, and place one small stem of celery in each glass as a garnish if desired.
- Serve at room temperature or chilled.

Yield: 2 (1-cup) servings

Calories: 44 (0% fat); Total Fat: 0 gm; Cholesterol: 0 mg; Carbohydrate: 11 gm; Dietary Fiber: 1 gm; Protein: 2 gm; Sodium: 35 mg
Diabetic Exchanges: 2 vegetables

Preparation time: 3 minutes or less

Menu Idea: This goes especially well with egg-based entrées such as omelets or frittatas. My Broccoli, Ham & Cheese Frittata (with only 8 carbs) on page 39 in *Busy People's Low-Fat Cookbook* is an excellent choice.

Sparkling Spiced Cider

The expense of purchasing those overpriced, nonalcoholic, sparkling beverages for special occasions got my creative wheels spinning. I can make the same amount for about one-tenth of the price the store retails it for. My husband and I like to have parties for two at home. (You know, no children, soft music, slow dancing.) This sparkling beverage is just the answer to his passion for nonalcoholic beverages that we can afford.

2 **cups cold water**	2 **cups sugar-free lemon-lime soda**
2 **(0.14-ounce) packets sugar-free spiced cider mix* (do not make as directed)**	

- Microwave the water for 2 minutes.
- Stir in the cider mix until it is completely dissolved.
- Stir in the soda.
- Serve chilled in pretty glasses.

*Note: The cider mix can be found in the tea and coffee sections of your local grocery store.

Yield: 4 (1-cup) servings

Calories: 8 (0% fat); Total Fat: 0 gm; Cholesterol: 0 mg; Carbohydrate: 2 gm; Dietary Fiber: 0 gm; Protein: 0 gm; Sodium: 35 mg
Diabetic Exchanges: Free

Preparation time: 2 minutes
Cooking time: 2 minutes
Total time: 4 minutes

Menu Idea: These are perfect for any special dinner party or when relaxing alone by the fireplace.

Apple Spiced Tea

This is good served hot in a teacup or cold over ice.

4 **tea bags**	8 **cinnamon sticks (optional)**
8 **cups water**	
3 **packets sugar-free, spiced apple cider mix**	

- Place the tea bags in the bottom of the pot of a coffee maker.
- Run the water through the coffee maker.
- Stir in the cider mix after all of the water has been heated.
- Let simmer 5 minutes.
- Pour into teacups, and garnish with a stick of cinnamon if desired.

Note: To serve chilled, simply remove the tea from the heat, and let cool to room temperature. Keep chilled in the refrigerator until ready to serve. Fill a glass with ice and pour the chilled tea over the ice. Do not pour the hot tea over the ice in the glass because it could make the glass break or crack.

Yield: 8 (1-cup) servings

Calories: 6 (0% fat); Total Fat: 0 gm; Cholesterol: 0 mg; Carbohydrate: 2 gm; Dietary Fiber: 0 gm; Protein: 0 gm; Sodium: 11 mg
Diabetic Exchanges: Free

Preparation time: 10 minutes or less

Menu Idea: Soothing and relaxing all by itself midday, morning, or evening. For an added special treat, serve with Honey Cookies (with only 6 carbs) on page 140 in *Busy People's Down-Home Cooking Without the Down-Home Fat.*

Spiced Ice Cubes

I make these for families when not everyone likes spiced tea. To solve the hassle of making two different teas and having two different kinds of tea in the refrigerator, now spiced tea lovers can pour our regular plain tea over these spiced ice cubes for the extra added flavor—no extra calories, no making different flavored teas.

1 **cup water**	1 **packet sugar-free, instant-spiced cider mix (10 packets to a box)**

- Cook the water in the microwave for 1 minute.
- Stir in the cider mix.
- Pour into ice cube trays, and freeze for about 1 hour or until frozen solid.

Variations: You can make different flavors using different sugar-free drink mixes.

Yield: 20 ice cubes (Use about 4 to 6 per tall glass of iced tea.)

Calories: 1 (0% fat); Total Fat: 0 gm; Cholesterol: 0 mg; Carbohydrate: 0 gm; Dietary Fiber: 0 gm; Protein: 0 gm; Sodium: 2 mg
Diabetic Exchanges: Free

Preparation time: 3 minutes or less

Menu Idea: These are a great way to spice up your iced tea.

Hot Mocha

This is undeniably some of the best low-carb mocha you will ever drink. A bonus is that it is a good source of protein as well.

1	cup hot water	3	cups fat-free, low-carb milk
2	tablespoons instant coffee (regular or decaffeinated is fine)	8	individual packets Splenda
			Dash of light salt (optional)
2	tablespoons cocoa powder		

- In a 2-quart saucepan over medium-low heat stir the water, coffee, cocoa, milk, Splenda, and salt until it is completely dissolved.
- Put a lid on the pan to quicken the heating process.
- Cook for 5 to 6 minutes, stirring occasionally.
- Serve hot.

Yield: 4 (1-cup) servings

Calories: 75 (0% fat); Total Fat: 0 gm; Cholesterol: 4 mg; Carbohydrate: 6 gm;
Dietary Fiber: 1 gm; Protein: 10 gm; Sodium: 158 mg
Diabetic Exchanges: $\frac{1}{2}$ skim milk, 1 very lean meat

Preparation time: 7 minutes or less

 **Menu Idea:** This terrific drink is just what the doctor ordered after being out in the cold. It will warm you all the way through to your bones. It goes well with the Cinnamon Stick Cookies on page 226 in this book.

Spiced Hot Chocolate

Be sure to drink the hot chocolate soon after it is prepared, because the ingredients settle to the bottom if it sits. The flavor is a spin-off of spiced chai tea.

4 cups fat-free, low-carb milk	1/2 cup Splenda Granular, measures like sugar
2 tablespoons cocoa powder	
1 teaspoon vanilla extract	1 teaspoon pumpkin pie spice

- In a nonstick saucepan heat the milk, cocoa, vanilla extract, Splenda, and pumpkin pie spice over medium heat, stirring frequently to prevent burning.
- Once the ingredients come to a low simmer, the beverage is ready to serve.

Yield: 4 (1-cup) servings

Calories: 97 (0% fat); Total Fat: 0 gm; Cholesterol: 5 mg; Carbohydrate: 8 gm;
Dietary Fiber: 1 gm; Protein: 13 gm; Sodium: 210 mg
Diabetic Exchanges: 1/2 skim milk, 1 1/2 very lean meat

Preparation time: 2 minutes
Cooking time: 3 minutes or less
Total time: 5 minutes or less

Menu Idea: Wonderful on a cold day with Cinnamon-Walnut Mini Drops on page 224 in this book.

Cinnamon & Spice Coffee

Now here's a special coffee you can deliver if you want to treat someone special to coffee in bed. This is a flavorful favorite.

2 **cups freshly brewed hot coffee**	2 **tablespoons fat-free, nondairy liquid creamer**
⅛ **teaspoon pumpkin pie spice**	**Dash of cinnamon**
5 **individual packets Splenda**	

- In a large 2-cup mug, stir together the hot coffee, pumpkin pie spice, Splenda, creamer, and cinnamon.
- Serve hot.

Yield: 1 (2-cup) serving

Calories: 27 (0% fat); Total Fat: 0 gm; Cholesterol: 0 mg; Carbohydrate: 6 gm; Dietary Fiber: 0 gm; Protein: 0 gm; Sodium: 2 mg
Diabetic Exchanges: ½ other carbohydrate

Preparation time: 10 minutes or less

Menu Idea: Great with Brown Sugar & Spice Sticks on page 217 in this book.

Coconut Cream Coffee

This is by far my favorite low-carb, fat-free, low-calorie, flavored coffee. You can make it with simple-to-find grocery store items that you most likely already have at home. Replacing my old high-calorie coffee with this delectable drink has made staying on the lower-carb lifestyle not only a lot easier for me, but it is also very delicious as well.

2 cups hot coffee	3 to 4 individual packets Splenda
1/2 teaspoon coconut flavoring, found near vanilla extract	2 tablespoons fat-free liquid creamer

- In a mug stir together the coffee, coconut flavoring, Splenda, and creamer until smooth and creamy.
- Drink hot or chilled over ice.

Yield: 1 (16-ounce) serving

Calories: 20 (0% fat); Total Fat: 0 gm; Cholesterol: 0 mg; Carbohydrate: 15 gm; Dietary Fiber: 0 gm; Protein: 0 gm; Sodium: 5 mg
Diabetic Exchanges: 1 other carbohydrate

Preparation time: 2 minutes or less

Menu Idea: This is just the answer in the morning with whatever I am having for breakfast. Some of my favorite low-carb breakfast recipes in this cookbook are Ham & Spinach Turnovers on page 200) and Broccoli, Ham & Cheddar Pies on page 198.

Cold Cappuccino Frothy

Each time I create a recipe, I grade it. This one got an A+. Try it, and I know you'll know why.

2	cups coffee, room temperature	7	individual packets Splenda
14	ice cubes	2	tablespoons fat-free, nondairy liquid creamer
1/8	teaspoon pumpkin pie spice		
1/2	cup fat-free, no-sugar-added frozen vanilla yogurt	I	teaspoon cocoa powder

- Put the coffee, ice, pumpkin pie spice, frozen yogurt, Splenda, creamer, and cocoa in a blender.
- Cover and process on the highest speed for 1 minute or until frothy.

Yield: 3 (1-cup) servings

Calories: 65 (0% fat); Total Fat: 0 gm; Cholesterol: 1 mg; Carbohydrate: 13 gm;
Dietary Fiber: 1 gm; Protein: 2 gm; Sodium: 7 mg
Diabetic Exchanges: 1 other carbohydrate

 **Preparation time:** 4 minutes or less

Menu Idea: On a hot day this refreshing drink is a nice change instead of hot coffee. The Sunrise Soufflé (with only 12 carbs), on page 22 in *Busy People's Slow Cooker Cookbook,* would be good with it too, because the slow cooker won't heat up your house.

Chocolate Frothy

This is best when you drink it right away, because the ingredients separate when sitting.

2 envelopes sugar-free hot chocolate mix (do not make as directed)	1/2 teaspoon vanilla extract
1 cup fat-free, low-carb milk	4 individual packets Splenda
1 cup ice cubes (about 7 ice cubes)	1 (1/4-ounce) envelope unflavored gelatin (do not make as directed)

- Put the hot chocolate mix, milk, ice, vanilla, Splenda, and gelatin mix in a blender, and process on high until thick and frothy, about 2 minutes.

Yield: 2½ (1-cup) servings

Calories: 46 (0% fat); Total Fat: 0 gm; Cholesterol: 2 mg; Carbohydrate: 3 gm; Dietary Fiber: 0 gm; Protein: 7 gm; Sodium: 90 mg
Diabetic Exchanges: 1 very lean meat

Preparation time: 4 minutes or less

Menu Idea: This wonderful chocolate beverage is a great low-carb substitute anytime you'd normally have a chocolate milkshake. For a sure cure of your chocolate cravings, serve with either the Chocolate Coconut Cookies (with 6 carbs) on page 234 or the Chocolate Sour Cream Cookies (with 6 carbs) on page 235, both from *Busy People's Diabetic Cookbook*.

Chocolate Monkey Frothy

If you like chocolate milkshakes you'll like this.

1 cup 2% reduced-fat, low-carb chocolate milk	2 tablespoons Splenda Granular, measures like sugar
1 cup ice cubes (about 7 ice cubes)	1 teaspoon cocoa powder
¹/₂ teaspoon imitation banana flavoring	Dash of salt (optional)

- In a blender put the milk, ice, banana flavoring, Splenda, and cocoa.
- Blend the ingredients on high for 1 to 2 minutes or until smooth and creamy.

Yield: 2 (1-cup) servings

Calories: 63 (33% fat); Total Fat: 2 gm; Cholesterol: 13 mg; Carbohydrate: 4 gm; Dietary Fiber: 1 gm; Protein: 6 gm; Sodium! 175 mg
Diabetic Exchanges: ¹/₂ other carbohydrate, 1 very lean meat

Preparation time: 3 minutes or less

Menu Idea: Wonderful with fat-free hot dogs on the grill and picnic items such as the Deviled Eggs on page 47 in *Busy People's Low-Fat Cookbook*.

Blueberry Frothy

Here's a wonderful way for people who aren't good about eating fruit to get their fruit in for the day.

½ teaspoon sugar-free tropical punch drink mix (do not make as directed)	**1 cup fat-free, low-carb milk**
	1 cup ice (about 7 ice cubes)
1 cup fresh blueberries	**2 individual packets Splenda**

- Put the drink mix, blueberries, milk, ice, and Splenda in a blender.
- Process on high for 1 to 2 minutes or until frothy.

Yield: 2½ (1-cup) servings

Calories: 66 (0% fat); Total Fat: 0 gm; Cholesterol: 2 mg; Carbohydrate: 10 gm;
Dietary Fiber: 1 gm; Protein: 5 gm; Sodium: 88 mg
Diabetic Exchanges: ½ fruit, 1 very lean meat

Preparation time: 5 minutes or less

Menu Idea: This beverage makes a grand meal replacement for breakfast on the run, because it is a healthy source of lean proteins and carbohydrates combined. However, if you want a little more protein, have a couple of pieces of "Fake Bacon" on page 30 in *Busy People's Low-Fat Cookbook.*

Lemonade Frothy

This extremely low-calorie treat will help you never miss high-calorie lemon beverages again. The gelatin not only helps make you feel full and satisfied, but it is also known to help strengthen nails.

20 sugar-free lemonade ice cubes*	2 (^{1}/4-ounce) envelopes unflavored gelatin
2 cups cold sugar-free lemonade	
2 to 4 individual packets Splenda (depending on how sweet you like it)	3 very thin lemon slices (optional)

- Put the lemonade-flavored ice cubes, lemonade, Splenda, and gelatin in a blender.
- Cover. Process on high for 1 minute or until slushy. The mixture will foam on top. That is fine.
- Pour into small glasses. If desired, garnish with a very thin wedge of lemon. (Cut a lemon into slices, cut a slit into the lemon slice, and set the slit on the rim of the glass.)

Note: Make a tray of lemonade ice cubes simply by filling an ice cube tray with sugar-free lemonade and freezing.

Yield: 3 (1-cup) servings

Calories: 25 (0% fat); Total Fat: 0 gm; Cholesterol: 0 mg; Carbohydrate: 1 gm; Dietary Fiber: 0 gm; Protein: 4 gm; Sodium: 9 mg
Diabetic Exchanges: ^{1}/2 very lean meat

Preparation time: 3 minutes or less

 **Menu Idea:** On a hot afternoon this tart, refreshing beverage is just the answer for a midday pick-me-up with a piece or two of extra-lean protein for a snack.

Breakaway Breakfasts & Breads

Sausage Biscuits

The savory flavors of Italian sausage are the stars of these hearty biscuits that men especially devour, and no one will ever guess they are vegetarian if you don't tell them.

1/2 cup fat-free whipped salad dressing	1 teaspoon baking soda
1 tablespoon Splenda Granular, measures like sugar	1 cup no-sugar-added applesauce
1 1/2 cups whole wheat flour	1 cup sausage-flavored Ground Meatless*

- Preheat the oven to 375 degrees.
- Spray two cookie sheets with nonfat cooking spray.
- In a medium-size mixing bowl stir together the whipped salad dressing, Splenda, flour, baking soda, applesauce, and Ground Meatless until well mixed. The dough will be slightly stiff.
- Drop by rounded tablespoonfuls onto the prepared cookie sheets.
- Bake for 13 minutes or until a toothpick inserted in the middle of a biscuit comes out clean.

Note: Ground Meatless is a vegetarian meat substitute made by Morningstar Farms. It's found in the freezer section of your grocery store. If desired you can use cooked and crumbled turkey Italian sausage instead, but the nutritional information will be different.

Yield: 18 (1-biscuit) servings

Calories: 54 (0% fat); Total Fat: 0 gm; Cholesterol: 0 mg; Carbohydrate: 10 gm; Dietary Fiber: 2 gm; Protein: 2 gm; Sodium: 157 mg
Diabetic Exchanges: 1/2 starch

Preparation time: 10 minutes
Cooking time: 13 minutes or less
Total time: 23 minutes or less

Menu Idea: Superb for breakfast sandwiches. Simply cut biscuits in half and fill the centers with cooked scrambled eggs.

Sour Cream Drop Biscuits

After you experience how super easy these are to make and how scrumptious they are to eat, you may never want to make any other type of biscuit again.

1 teaspoon baking soda	1¹/₂ cups whole wheat flour
1 cup fat-free sour cream	¹/₄ cup fat-free whipped salad dressing
¹/₂ cup no-sugar-added applesauce	
¹/₄ cup Splenda Granular, measures like sugar	

- Preheat the oven to 375 degrees.
- Spray two cookie sheets with nonfat cooking spray.
- In a medium-size mixing bowl stir together the baking soda, sour cream, applesauce, Splenda, flour, and salad dressing until well mixed. Dough will be slightly stiff.
- Drop onto the prepared cookie sheets by rounded tablespoonfuls.
- Bake for 11 to 13 minutes.

Yield: 24 (1-biscuit) servings

Calories: 43 (0% fat); Total Fat: 0 gm; Cholesterol: 2 mg; Carbohydrate: 9 gm; Dietary Fiber: 1 gm; Protein: 2 gm; Sodium: 82 mg
Diabetic Exchanges: ¹/₂ starch

Preparation time: 10 minutes or less
Cooking time: 13 minutes or less
Total time: 23 minutes or less

Menu Idea: Super terrific for any meal any time. Eat for breakfast with the Cream Cheese & Crab Frittata on page 171 or for lunch with the Zesty Soup on page 93 or for dinner with the Salisbury Steak with Mushroom Gravy on page 205, all in this book.

Bran Muffin Bites

Bakeries are selling mini muffins called muffin bites. That clever idea made me decide to give my own version a try. Every muffin that was made was gone the next morning when my fifteen-year-old daughter had a sleepover. So I know they were a hit with the teens. These are best eaten the day they are made.

2 plus 2 cups oat bran cereal flakes	1 cup fat-free, low-carb milk
2 egg whites	2 tablespoons no-sugar-added applesauce
2 teaspoons baking powder	1 tablespoon dark brown sugar
$^1/_2$ cup Splenda Granular, measures like sugar	

- Preheat the oven to 425 degrees.
- Spray two 24 mini muffin tins with nonfat cooking spray. Set aside.
- In a food processor grind 2 cups bran flakes into a flour consistency.
- In a small bowl beat the egg whites until soft peaks form.
- In a medium-size mixing bowl stir together the cereal (both the flakes and ground-up cereal) and the baking powder.
- To the cereal mixture add the Splenda, milk, applesauce, dark brown sugar, and egg whites just enough to moisten the dry ingredients. Let sit for 1 minute.
- Put 1 rounded tablespoonful of the mix into each mini muffin cup.
- Bake for 8 to 10 minutes or until toothpick inserted in the middle of a muffin comes out clean.

Yield: 16 (3-muffin) servings

Calories: 50 (0% fat); Total Fat: 0 gm; Cholesterol: 0 mg; Carbohydrate: 10 gm; Dietary Fiber: 1 gm; Protein: 2 gm; Sodium: 159 mg
Diabetic Exchanges: $^1/_2$ starch

Preparation time: 10 minutes
Cooking time: 13 minutes
Total time: 23 minutes

Menu Idea: I ate four of these for a quickie breakfast with a cup of the Tomato Juice Cooler (page 33 of this book), and the meal was quite satisfying.

Cinnamon & Spice Apple Muffin Bites

These are slightly sweet, slightly tart, and an absolutely wonderful comfort food served warm. I'm amazed at how delicious these are even though they are low-carb and low-calorie.

1/4 cup applesauce	1 cup whole wheat flour
1 cup Splenda Granular, measures like sugar	1 teaspoon pumpkin pie spice
1/2 cup fat-free mayonnaise	1 (15-ounce) can apple slices, drained and cut into tiny pieces (not pie filling)
1 teaspoon baking soda	

- Preheat the oven to 375 degrees.
- Spray mini-muffin tins with nonfat cooking spray.
- In a medium-size mixing bowl stir together with a spatula the applesauce, Splenda, mayonnaise, baking soda, flour, and pumpkin pie spice until well mixed.
- Gently stir in the apples.
- Fill the mini-muffin tins two-thirds full, about 1½ tablespoons.
- Bake for 12 minutes or until a toothpick inserted in the middle of a muffin comes out clean.
- Let the muffins sit a couple of minutes before serving.

Yield: 22 (1-muffin) servings

Calories: 37 (0% fat); Total Fat: 0 gm; Cholesterol: 1 mg; Carbohydrate: 8 gm; Dietary Fiber: 1 gm; Protein: 1 gm; Sodium: 102 mg
Diabetic Exchanges: ½ starch

Preparation time: 10 minutes
Cooking time: 12 minutes or less
Total time: 22 minutes or less

Menu Idea: Enjoy three of these muffin bites along with a cup of low-carb milk for a nutritious and delicious breakfast or midday snack.

Blueberry Muffin Bites

I can't imagine the low-carb diet being any tastier than these fabulous muffins.

1/2 cup fat-free mayonnaise	1 teaspoon baking soda
1 cup plus 1 tablespoon Splenda Granular, measures like sugar	1 1/2 cups whole wheat flour
	1 teaspoon ground cinnamon
1 cup no-sugar-added applesauce	1 cup fresh blueberries, cleaned

- Preheat the oven to 375 degrees.
- Spray mini-muffin tins with nonfat cooking spray.
- In a medium-size mixing bowl stir with a spatula the mayonnaise, 1 cup Splenda, applesauce, baking soda, flour, and cinnamon until well mixed.
- Very gently stir in the blueberries.
- Fill the mini-muffin tins two-thirds full, about 1 1/2 tablespoons.
- Sprinkle the tops of the muffins very lightly with the remaining 1 tablespoon Splenda before baking.
- Bake for 10 to 12 minutes or until a toothpick inserted in the middle of a muffin comes out clean.
- Let the muffins sit a couple of minutes before serving.

Yield: 26 (1-muffin) servings

Calories: 38 (0% fat); Total Fat: 0 gm; Cholesterol: 0 mg; Carbohydrate: 9 gm;
Dietary Fiber: 1 gm; Protein: 1 gm; Sodium: 86 mg
Diabetic Exchanges: 1/2 starch

Preparation time: 10 minutes
Cooking time: 13 minutes or less
Total time: 23 minutes or less

Menu Idea: These are a nice way to start your day with the Puffy Seafood Omelet on page 58 in this book.

Peaches & Spice Muffin Bites

These muffins melt-in your-mouth with sweet, country-time goodness. Georgia peaches never had it so good in a low-fat, low-carb muffin.

1 fresh, ripe peach, cut into 1/4-inch pieces (about 1 cup)	1 teaspoon baking soda
1 cup plus 2 tablespoons Splenda Granular, measures like sugar	1 1/2 cups whole wheat flour
1/2 cup fat-free mayonnaise	1 plus 1 teaspoon ground pumpkin pie spice or ground cinnamon
1 cup no-sugar-added cinnamon-flavored applesauce	

- Preheat the oven to 375 degrees.
- Spray mini-muffin tins with nonfat cooking spray.
- In a medium bowl gently toss the peaches with 2 tablespoons Splenda.
- In another medium-size mixing bowl stir together with a spatula the remaining 1 cup Splenda, the mayonnaise, applesauce, baking soda, flour, and 1 teaspoon ground pumpkin pie spice until well blended.
- Fill the mini-muffin tins two-thirds full.
- Sprinkle the tops of muffins very lightly with the remaining 1 teaspoon pumpkin pie spice before baking.
- Bake for 11 to 13 minutes or until a toothpick inserted in the middle of a muffin comes out clean.
- Let the muffins sit a couple of minutes before serving.

Yield: 28 (1-muffin) servings

Calories: 34 (0% fat); Total Fat: 0 gm; Cholesterol: 0 mg; Carbohydrate: 8 gm; Dietary Fiber: 1 gm; Protein: 1 gm; Sodium: 80 mg
Diabetic Exchanges: 1/2 starch

Preparation time: 10 minutes
Cooking time: 13 minutes or less
Total time: 23 minutes or less

Menu Idea: Try these wonderful muffins with the Cream Cheese & Crab Frittata on page 171 in this book.

Whole Wheat Muffin Bites

I am absolutely thrilled how moist and scrumptious these muffins are. I honestly don't think they could get any better.

¹/2 cup fat-free mayonnaise	1 teaspoon baking soda
1 cup Splenda Granular, measures like sugar	1 teaspoon ground cinnamon
1 cup no-sugar-added applesauce	1¹/2 cups whole wheat flour

- Preheat the oven to 375 degrees.
- Spray mini-muffin tins with nonfat cooking spray.
- In a medium-size mixing bowl with electric mixer beat on medium speed the mayonnaise, Splenda, applesauce, baking soda, and cinnamon until well blended.
- Add the flour. Blend until thoroughly mixed.
- Pour 1¹/2 tablespoons of the muffin mix into each of the prepared muffin tins.
- Bake for 10 to 12 minutes or until a toothpick inserted in the center of a muffin comes out clean.

Yield: 9 (3-muffin) servings

Calories: 101 (7% fat); Total Fat: 1 gm; Cholesterol: 1 mg; Carbohydrate: 22 gm; Dietary Fiber: 3 gm; Protein: 3 gm; Sodium: 248 mg
Diabetic Exchanges: 1¹/2 starch

Preparation time: 15 minutes
Cooking time: 12 minutes or less
Total time: 27 minutes or less

Menu Idea: These are good for breakfast, snacks, or even with an entrée. For breakfast or brunch serve these muffins with the Puffy Seafood Omelet on page 58 in this book.

Breakfast Sausage & Egg Cups

My girlfriend's children really liked this recipe and gobbled them all up before we could look twice.

3 cups sausage-flavored Ground Meatless*	**1 tablespoon dried chives (optional)**
³/4 cup fat-free mozzarella cheese	**Light salt and pepper**
3 cups liquid egg substitute	

- Preheat the oven to 350 degrees.
- Spray a 12-cup, regular-size muffin tin with nonfat cooking spray.

For each muffin cup:

- Put ¼ cup Ground Meatless in the bottom.
- Put 1 tablespoon cheese over the Ground Meatless.
- Pour ¼ cup egg substitute over the cheese.
- Sprinkle the top with ¼ teaspoon chives, if desired.
- Sprinkle lightly with the salt and pepper, if desired.
- Bake in the preheated oven for 15 to 20 minutes, or until the eggs are fully cooked.

*Note: Ground Meatless is a vegetarian meat substitute made by Morningstar Farms. It's found in the freezer section of your grocery store. If desired you can use cooked and crumbled turkey Italian sausage instead, but the nutritional information will be different.

Variation: Bacon and Cheddar Breakfast Egg Cups: Substitute 1 tablespoon 30% less fat real bacon pieces for the sausage and cheddar cheese for the mozzarella cheese.

Yield: 12 (1-egg cup) servings

Calories: 76 (0% fat); Total Fat: 0 gm; Cholesterol: 1 mg; Carbohydrate: 4 gm; Dietary Fiber: 2 gm; Protein: 14 gm; Sodium: 310 mg
Diabetic Exchanges: 2 very lean meat

Preparation time: 5 minutes
Cooking time: 15 to 20 minutes
Total time: 25 minutes

Menu Idea: Drinking the Tomato Juice Cocktail (on page 34 of this book) will complete this light breakfast with healthy carbohydrates.

Meat Lovers' Breakfast Soft Taco

The only two things that resemble a taco are the soft tortilla and the shape of this breakfast sandwich; but I tell you, this is awfully good.

1/4 cup liquid egg substitute	1 rounded teaspoon 30% less fat, real bacon bits
1 rounded tablespoon sausage-flavored Ground Meatless*	1/2 (10-inch) low-carb flour tortilla
1 rounded tablespoon diced, extra-lean ham	

- Spray a cereal bowl with nonfat cooking spray and add the egg, Ground Meatless, ham, and bacon bits. Beat together with a fork until well mixed.
- Cover with wax paper and cook in a carousel microwave for 1 1/2 minutes.
- Fold the flour tortilla in half and pop it in the toaster for about 30 seconds.
- Lift the egg-meat mixture with a fork to assure it is completely cooked before transferring it to the heated tortilla.
- Fold the toasted tortilla in half around the cooked egg and meat. Serve hot.

Note: Ground Meatless is a vegetarian meat substitute made by Morningstar Farms. It's found in the freezer section of your grocery store. If desired you can use cooked and crumbled turkey Italian sausage instead, but the nutritional information will be different.

Yield: 1 serving

Calories: 118 (28% fat); Total Fat: 4 gm; Cholesterol: 10 mg; Carbohydrate: 8 gm; Dietary Fiber: 3 gm; Protein: 14 gm; Sodium: 550 mg
Diabetic Exchanges: 1/2 starch, 1 1/2 lean meat

Preparation time: 1 minute or less
Cooking time: 1 1/2 minutes
Total time: 3 minutes or less

Menu Idea: This is a terrific meal to eat on the run, because it is not messy and travels well. I recommend a small piece of fruit, such as a pear, and a cup of coffee to round off this meal.

Puffy Seafood Omelet

You'll love how easy this recipe is. Your dining guests will savor the flavor.

10 **egg whites**	8 **ounces imitation crabmeat, cut into bite-size pieces (1½ cups)**
½ **cup fat-free shredded mozzarella cheese**	8 **ounces salad shrimp (2 cups)**
½ **teaspoon garlic salt**	½ **cup cocktail sauce**

- Preheat the oven to 375 degrees.
- In a large bowl beat the egg whites with an electric mixer on high speed until stiff peaks form.
- With a spatula, gently stir the cheese, garlic salt, crabmeat, and shrimp into the beaten egg whites until well blended.
- Generously spray a nonstick, 12-inch skillet with nonfat cooking spray. Preheat the skillet to medium on the stove.
- Pour the egg mixture into the prepared skillet. Do not stir.
- For about 10 minutes, cook undisturbed or until the bottom is firm.
- Once the bottom is firm, transfer the entire skillet to the oven and bake for 8 to 10 minutes. After 10 minutes, turn the omelet over in the skillet and continue baking another 2 minutes, or until it is soft-set and slightly firm, but not dry.
- Remove from the oven, spread the top with the cocktail sauce, and cut into six pie-shape pieces.

Yield: 6 servings

Calories: 135 (8% fat); Total Fat: 1 gm; Cholesterol: 83 mg; Carbohydrate: 9 gm; Dietary Fiber: 1 gm; Protein: 22 gm; Sodium: 825 mg
Diabetic Exchanges: ½ other carbohydrate, 3 very lean meat

Preparation time: 8 minutes or less
Cooking time: 22 minutes
Total time: 30 minutes or less

Menu Idea: Sour Cream Drop Biscuits on page 50 of this book are tasty with this.

Awesome
Appetizers

Ham & Cheese Pastry Roll-Ups

These crispy treats are incredible straight from the oven. It is hard to believe they are low-fat and low-calorie because they are so fantastic.

¹/₂ (16-ounce) box phyllo (filo) dough (10 sheets)	16 ounces extra lean, very thinly sliced honey ham
16 ounces shredded fat-free Cheddar cheese	¹/₂ cup grated Parmesan cheese

- Preheat the oven to 350 degrees.
- Spray two cookie sheets with nonfat cooking spray.
- Cut the phyllo dough in half to make two 13 x 9-inch rectangles.
- Use only half a sheet of phyllo dough at a time. Cover the remaining sheets to be used with a very slightly damp cloth so they don't dry out.
- Lightly sprinkle 1 tablespoon shredded cheddar cheese near the short edge of one of the ends of the phyllo dough.
- Add two thin slices of ham and roll very tightly.
- Spray the outside of the roll with nonfat cooking spray to help seal. Sprinkle the top with ½ teaspoon grated Parmesan cheese and cut in half.
- Repeat with the remaining phyllo sheets, and place all the rolls on a prepared cookie sheet seam side down. Do not let them touch each other.
- Bake for 5 to 7 minutes or until golden brown.

Yield: 40 (1-roll) servings

Calories: 55 (18% fat); Total Fat: 1 gm; Cholesterol: 9 mg; Carbohydrate: 4 gm; Dietary Fiber: 0 gm; Protein: 7 gm; Sodium: 288 mg
Diabetic Exchanges: ½ starch, 1 very lean meat

Preparation time: 23 minutes or less
Cooking time: 7 minutes or less
Total time: 30 minutes or less

Menu Idea: These great little roll-ups are perfect for something special with soups or salads instead of sandwiches. Try them with the Chicken Asparagus Soup (with only 6 carbs) on page 48 in *Busy People's Slow Cooker Cookbook*.

Honey Mustard Ham Roll-Ups

These cocktail size, mini roll-up sandwiches are huge hits at parties.

1/4 cup light whipped salad dressing	6 fat-free, low-carb tortillas
1 tablespoon mustard	3/4 cup shredded fat-free Cheddar cheese
1 individual packet Splenda	1/2 pound thinly sliced, deli-style honey ham
2 tablespoons finely chopped red onion	

- In a small bowl mix the salad dressing, mustard, Splenda, and onion together until well mixed.

For each tortilla:

- Spread 1 tablespoon of the mixture on each tortilla.
- Sprinkle with 2 tablespoons cheese.
- Press the ham onto the cheese.
- Microwave each tortilla for 30 seconds.
- Roll up tightly and secure with toothpicks.
- Cut each tortilla wrap into 3 pieces.

Yield: 18 servings

Calories: 68 (36% fat); Total Fat: 3 gm; Cholesterol: 8 mg; Carbohydrate: 6 gm; Dietary Fiber: 2 gm; Protein: 6 gm; Sodium: 353 mg
Diabetic Exchanges: 1/2 starch, 1/2 lean meat

Preparation time: 10 minutes

Menu Idea: For a party of low-carb items, serve these foods from *Busy People's Diabetic Cookbook:* Smoked Sausage Cheese Spread on page 107, Shrimp Spread on page 111, and Hawaiian Chicken Spread on page 108. Use fresh celery sticks, bell pepper strips, and cucumber slices instead of crackers.

Italian Roll-Ups

I love eating these not only as an appetizer but also as a meal. Because they taste so good I don't want to wait till my next party to serve them as an appetizer. Matter of fact, I ate some today for lunch. They are quick and easy to put together and A+ in flavor.

2 tablespoons fat-free Italian salad dressing	2 tablespoons red bell pepper, finely chopped
1 low-carb flour tortilla	2 tablespoons fat-free mozzarella cheese
2 tablespoons sausage-flavored, Ground Meatless* crumbles	

- Spread the Italian salad dressing on the flour tortilla.
- Sprinkle the Ground Meatless, bell pepper, and mozzarella cheese on top of the dressing and microwave for 25 to 30 seconds.
- Roll like a jelly roll. Let it sit for a minute to allow the tortilla to absorb the juices and fabulous flavors.
- With the seam facing down, cut into four pieces.

Yield: 2 (2-piece) servings

*Note: Ground Meatless is a vegetarian meat substitute made by Morningstar Farms. It's found in the freezer section of your grocery store. If desired, you can use cooked and crumbled turkey Italian sausage instead, but the nutritional information will be different.

Calories: 82 (27% fat); Total Fat: 3 gm; Cholesterol: 2 mg; Carbohydrate: 10 gm; Dietary Fiber: 3 gm; Protein: 7 gm; Sodium: 500 mg
Diabetic Exchanges: 1/2 starch, 1 lean meat

Preparation time: 5 minutes or less
Cooking time: 1 minute or less
Total time: 6 minutes or less

Menu Idea: As an appetizer they are especially good on Italian-themed buffets with items such as Italian Dip (with only 7 carbs) on page 15 in *Busy People's Down-Home Cooking Without the Down-Home Fat* cookbook or as an entrée with a cup of soup such as New-Fashioned Soup (with only 8 carbs) on page 56 in *Busy People's Slow Cooker Cookbook.*

Weenie Wraps with Cheese

We had these as an entrée for a small birthday party luncheon I had for a friend instead of sandwiches or salads, and they were a huge hit. However, they also make great appetizers for buffets as well.

1	pound fat-free wieners or 1 (14-ounce) package low-fat smoked sausage	2½ full sheets (or 5 half sheets) phyllo dough*, cut into 1 x 13-inch-long strips
2	slices fat-free American or Cheddar cheese, cut into 12 thin pieces	

- Preheat the oven to 400 degrees.
- Coat one large cookie sheet with nonfat cooking spray.
- Cut the wieners into thirds (or the sausage links into quarters lengthwise. Then cut the quartered sausages into thirds.)
- Roll each small piece of wiener (or sausage) and cheese strip in one of the phyllo dough strips.
- Spray the end of the phyllo strip with nonfat cooking spray. It will seal the seam closed.
- Place the wrap seam side down on a prepared cookie sheet.
- Continue until all of the wiener (or sausage) pieces and cheese strips are used. Discard any remaining phyllo dough.
- Lightly spray all of the tops of the weenie wraps with nonfat cooking spray.
- Bake for 7 to 8 minutes or until crisp and lightly browned.

Note: Phyllo dough sheets are super easy to work with and come in a 16-ounce box. There are either 2 (8-ounce) packages of half sheets or 1 (16-ounce) package of full sheets within the 16-ounce box of phyllo dough sheets. They are in the freezer section with dessert products.

Yield: 24 appetizer servings (1 per serving)

(with sausage) Calories: 31 (16% fat); Total Fat: 1 gm; Cholesterol: 6 mg; Carbohydrate: 4 gm; Dietary Fiber: 0 gm; Protein: 3 gm; Sodium: 174 mg
Diabetic Exchanges: ½ starch
(with fat-free wieners) Calories: 23 (0% fat); Total Fat: 0 gm; Cholesterol: 6 mg; Carbohydrate: 3 gm; Dietary Fiber: 0 gm; Protein: 3 gm; Sodium: 217 mg
Diabetic Exchanges: ½ starch

Yield: 6 entrée servings (4 per serving)

(with sausage) Calories: 123 (16% fat); Total Fat: 2 gm; Cholesterol: 25 mg; Carbohydrate: 14 gm; Dietary Fiber: 0 gm; Protein: 10 gm; Sodium: 695 mg Diabetic Exchanges: 1 starch, 1 very lean meat
(with fat-free wieners) Calories: 93 (0% fat); Total Fat: 0 gm; Cholesterol: 24 mg; Carbohydrate: 10 gm; Dietary Fiber: 0 gm; Protein: 11 gm; Sodium: 869 mg Diabetic Exchanges: 1 starch, 1 very lean meat

Preparation time: 15 minutes
Cooking time: 8 minutes or less
Total time: 23 minutes or less

Menu Idea: The Watermelon Slushy (on page 28 in this book) along with the Red Wine Cucumber Slices (on page 49 in *Busy People's Down-Home Cooking Without the Down-Home Fat*) served with these Weenie Wraps make a great summertime meal.

Fiesta Cups

These are crispy and spicy all-in-one appetizers.

1 (12-ounce) bag sausage-flavored, Ground Meatless*	4 ounces fat-free cream cheese, cubed
1 (1.25-ounce) packet taco seasoning (do not make as directed)	2 (2.1-ounce) boxes mini phyllo shells (found in freezer section with pastries)
1 (14-ounce) can diced tomatoes with green chilies, do not drain	1/4 cup fat-free shredded Cheddar cheese

- Preheat the oven to 350 degrees.
- Place the phyllo shells on a cookie sheet that has been coated with nonfat cooking spray.
- In a 12-inch, nonstick skillet cook the Ground Meatless with the taco seasoning mix and diced tomatoes over medium heat. Bring to a low boil and let simmer for 5 minutes, stirring occasionally. As the mixture cooks, some of the moisture will evaporate.
- Drain and discard any remaining liquid from the Ground Meatless. Stir in the cream cheese and continue cooking until the cheese is completely melted.
- Put 2 teaspoons of the mixture into each of the mini phyllo shells.
- Sprinkle the tops lightly with shredded cheese, bake for 5 minutes and serve hot.

Note: Ground Meatless is a vegetarian meat substitute made by Morningstar Farms. It's found in the freezer section of your grocery store. If desired, you can use cooked and crumbled turkey Italian sausage instead, but the nutritional information will be different.

Yield: 15 (2-shell) servings

Calories: 98 (34% fat); Total Fat: 4 gm; Cholesterol: 2 mg; Carbohydrate: 9 gm;
Dietary Fiber: 1 gm; Protein: 7 gm; Sodium: 479 mg
Diabetic Exchanges: $\frac{1}{2}$ starch, 1 lean meat

Preparation time: 10 minutes or less
Cooking time: 12 minutes or less
Total time: 22 minutes or less

Menu Idea: These are fantastic for Mexican-theme buffets or parties when only appetizers are being served. For a festive lunch, serve with Summer Fiesta Salad on page 42 in *Busy People's Down-Home Cooking Without the Down-Home Fat*.

Pork Pastry Squares

My mouth waters thinking about how scrumptious these are. They are so delectable.

4 ounces extra lean ham, diced (approximately I cup)	2 (8-ounce) packages fat-free shredded mozzarella cheese
¼ cup 30% less fat, real bacon bits	I (16-ounce) box (20 sheets) phyllo dough sheets (found in freezer section)
¼ cup dried parsley	
I cup sausage-flavored, Ground Meatless crumbles*	½ cup reduced-fat, finely shredded Cheddar cheese

- Preheat the oven to 350 degrees.
- Coat a 9 x 13-inch pan with nonfat cooking spray.
- In a medium-size bowl stir together the ham, bacon bits, parsley, sausage crumbles, and mozzarella cheese until well mixed.
- Cut the phyllo dough in half to make two 9 x 13-inch stacks. Wrap up one stack to save for a later use.
- (Step A) Take 1 layer of phyllo dough, and place it in the bottom of the prepared pan. Spray the top of the dough sheet with nonfat cooking spray.
- (Step B) Place a second layer of phyllo dough on top of the first. Once again, spray the top with nonfat cooking spray.
- (Step C) Continue repeating until you have used 7 sheets of phyllo.
- (Step D) Spread 1½ cups of the meat mixture over the dough.
- Repeat steps A through D two more times.
- Sprinkle the top layer with cheddar cheese.
- Cover with aluminum foil and bake for 15 minutes.
- Remove the foil. Increase the temperature of the oven to 400 degrees and bake for another 5 minutes.
- Let cool for 5 minutes before cutting into 24 pieces.

Note: Ground Meatless is a vegetarian meat substitute made by Morningstar Farms. It's found in the freezer section of your grocery store. If desired, you can use cooked and crumbled turkey Italian sausage instead, but the nutritional information will be different.

Yield: 24 appetizer servings (1 per serving)

Calories: 84 (15% fat); Total Fat: 1 gm; Cholesterol: 9 mg; Carbohydrate: 8 gm; Dietary Fiber: 1 gm; Protein: 10 gm; Sodium: 393 mg
Diabetic Exchanges: $\frac{1}{2}$ starch, 1 very lean meat

Yield: 6 entrée servings (4 per serving)

Calories: 336 (15% fat); Total Fat: 5 gm; Cholesterol: 35 mg; Carbohydrate: 32 gm; Dietary Fiber: 4 gm; Protein: 38 gm; Sodium: 1573 mg
Diabetic Exchanges: 2 starch, 4 very lean meat

Preparation time: 10 minutes or less
Cooking time: 20 minutes
Total time: 30 minutes or less

Menu Idea: This appetizer tastes so fantastic I could make a meal out of it. Four of these appetizers make a nice size entrée. As an entrée, a fresh vegetable salad such as the Greek-Style Cucumber Salad on page 118 or the Red Lettuce Salad on page 113, both in this book, would be delicious accompaniments.

Crabby Shells

Don't let the grouchy recipe name turn you away from their fabulous flavor. You have to try these at least once. They are so good. I even like them served chilled the next day for lunch. They are not as crispy, but the flavor is still good.

4 ounces fat-free cream cheese	1 teaspoon Splenda Granular, measures like sugar
1 tablespoon fat-free, whipped salad dressing	1 (2.1-ounce) box baked mini phyllo shells (found in frozen dessert section)
4 ounces imitation crab leg meat, shredded into tiny pieces	
1 plus ½ teaspoons chopped dried chives	

- Preheat the oven to 350 degrees.
- Coat a cookie sheet with nonfat cooking spray.
- In a bowl stir together the cream cheese, salad dressing, crabmeat, 1 teaspoon chives, and Splenda until smooth and creamy.
- Put 1½ to 2 teaspoons of the mixture into each mini shell. Very lightly sprinkle the tops of the stuffed mini shells with the remaining ½ teaspoon chives.
- Cover the shells with aluminum foil.
- Bake for 5 minutes or until fully heated.
- Let sit a couple of minutes to cool before serving.

Yield: 15 mini stuffed shells (1 per serving)

Calories: 36 (34% fat); Total Fat: 1 gm; Cholesterol: 3 mg; Carbohydrate: 3 gm; Dietary Fiber: 0 gm; Protein: 2 gm; Sodium: 121 mg
Diabetic Exchanges: ½ starch

Preparation time: 10 minutes or less
Cooking time: 5 minutes
Total time: 15 minutes or less

Menu Idea: Great as an appetizer for a fish-based entrée such as Sautéed Scallops with Garlic (with only 3 carbs) on page 180 in *Busy People's Diabetic Cookbook.*

Stuffed Cucumber Slices

Don't limit yourself to this clever idea with this filling only. Use any of the many other mouth-watering cream cheese spreads in the appetizer section of this book to stuff cucumbers with as well.

1	large cucumber, washed (do not peel)	1	teaspoon dried chives or 2 teaspoons chopped fresh chives
2	ounces fat-free cream cheese	1	(2.5-ounce) package chipped beef, finely chopped
½	teaspoon ranch salad dressing mix (do not make as directed)		

- With a long, sharp knife, cut off the ends of the cucumber and discard. With a knife or a spoon remove and discard the seeds from the center of the cucumber without slicing the cucumber. Set the hollowed-out cucumber aside.
- In a medium bowl with a spatula, stir together the cream cheese, ranch salad dressing mix, chives, and chipped beef until well mixed.
- Press the cream cheese mixture into the center of cucumber, filling it completely.
- With a very sharp knife, cut the stuffed cucumber into ½-inch-thick slices.
- Keep chilled until ready to serve.

Yield: 6 (3-slice) servings

Calories: 66 (25% fat); Total Fat: 2 gm; Cholesterol: 19 mg; Carbohydrate: 4 gm; Dietary Fiber: 1 gm; Protein: 8 gm; Sodium: 511 mg
Diabetic Exchanges: 1 vegetable, 1 lean meat

Preparation time: 10 minutes or less

Menu Idea: These crunchy treats are super for a snack on a hot day with a refreshing Orange Slushy (only 10 carbohydrates) on page 203 in *Busy People's Down-Home Cooking Without the Down-Home Fat.*

Stuffed Cherry Tomatoes

The time-consuming thing about making these is preparing and stuffing the cherry tomatoes. I don't usually take a half hour to prepare an appetizer or side vegetable dish. However, for a clever appetizer or vegetable side dish or snack for a special occasion, the extra time is worth the investment.

1	pint large cherry tomatoes	1	tablespoon fat-free mayonnaise
8	ounces fat-free cream cheese, softened	1/4	cup fat-free shredded Cheddar cheese
1	tablespoon dried chives	1/4	cup finely chopped, extra lean ham
1/2	teaspoon celery salt		

- With a very sharp knife, cut the tops off all the tomatoes.
- With a grapefruit spoon (a teaspoon works okay as well), scoop out the inside of each tomato. Set the hollowed-out tomatoes aside to drain. Discard the tomato tops and insides.
- In a medium-size bowl with a spatula, stir together the cream cheese, chives, celery salt, mayonnaise, cheese, and ham until well mixed.
- Put ½ teaspoon ham and cheese mixture into each tomato.
- Serve chilled.

Yield: 12 servings (4 per serving)

Calories: 37 (0% fat); Total Fat: 0 gm; Cholesterol: 5 mg; Carbohydrate: 3 gm; Dietary Fiber: 0 gm; Protein: 4 gm; Sodium: 206 mg
Diabetic Exchanges: ½ very lean meat

Preparation time: 30 minutes or less

Menu Ideas: These are an appetizer just right for special outdoor cookouts or barbeques. They are also a nice alternative to a vegetable side dish for special picnics or a ladies' tea or brunch.

Stuffed Celery Sticks

A terrific blend of crunchy and creamy textures.

4	ounces fat-free cream cheese	I	tablespoon fat-free whipped salad dressing
I	tablespoon honey Dijon mustard	1/4	cup fat-free shredded Cheddar cheese
I	tablespoon fresh chives or 2 teaspoons dried chives (optional)	4	ounces ham, finely diced *
		8	long stalks celery, cleaned

- In a medium bowl mix together the cream cheese, mustard, chives (optional), and whipped salad dressing until smooth and creamy.
- Stir in the cheese and ham until well mixed.
- Spread into the celery stalks.
- Cut the stuffed celery into 3-inch lengths.

Note: To save time, buy the ham already diced.

Yield: 8 (2-piece) servings

Calories: 51 (19% fat); Total Fat: 1 gm; Cholesterol: 11 mg; Carbohydrate: 3 gm; Dietary Fiber: 0 gm; Protein: 6 gm; Sodium: 360 mg
Diabetic Exchanges: 1 very lean meat

Preparation time: 15 minutes or less

Menu Idea: For a light lunch, have a salad with your favorite low-carb dressing and four Stuffed Celery Sticks on the side along with Butter Rum Spiced Cider (with only 5 carbs) on page 61 in *Busy People's Diabetic Cookbook.*

Vanilla Cream Cheese

I got this idea from a popular bagel restaurant. Once again, I liked the flavor, but I refuse to pay for something that is overpriced and is high in fat and calories when I can make it at a fraction of the price and with a fraction of the fat, calories, and carbohydrates. You are going to like this every bit as much as I do. I just know it.

4 ounces fat-free cream cheese, softened	1/2 teaspoon vanilla extract
4 individual packets Splenda	

- In a small container mix together the cream cheese, Splenda, and vanilla extract until well blended.
- Cover and keep refrigerated until ready to use.

Yield: 8 (1-tablespoon) servings

Calories: 18 (0% fat); Total Fat: 0 gm; Cholesterol: 2 mg; Carbohydrate: 2 gm; Dietary Fiber: 0 gm; Protein: 2 gm; Sodium: 70 mg
Diabetic Exchanges: Free

Preparation time: 5 minutes or less

Menu Idea: Great on low-carb bagels, low-carb crackers, or as a spread on celery.

Lemon Cream Spread

This is just the right answer for midday teas or snacks when you want to relax and enjoy a small treat that's low-carb, low-fat, and low-calorie, too. Tell me, does it get any better than that?

4 ounces fat-free cream cheese	**¹/₈ teaspoon sugar-free lemonade**
I individual packet Splenda	**mix (do not make as directed)**

- Mix the cream cheese, Splenda, and lemonade mix together until smooth and creamy.
- Keep chilled in an airtight container until ready to eat.

Yield: 8 (1-tablespoon) servings

Calories: 15 (0% fat); Total Fat: 0 gm; Cholesterol: 2 mg; Carbohydrate: 1 gm;
Dietary Fiber: 0 gm; Protein: 2 gm; Sodium: 70 mg
Diabetic Exchanges: Free

 Preparation time: 2 minutes or less

 **Menu Idea:** This is a perfect smooth and creamy spread for low-carb crackers or bagels when you want something just a little sweet without a lot of calories to curb your sweet tooth.

Crab Dip & Spread

This is good stuffed in celery or cherry tomatoes, and also good on low-carbohydrate crackers.

1 (6-ounce) can real crabmeat, do not drain	1 tablespoon chopped fresh chives or green onion tops (or 2 teaspoons dried chives)
4 ounces fat-free cream cheese	1/2 teaspoon imitation butter flavoring (found near vanilla extract)
1 tablespoon minced garlic	
1/4 cup fat-free mozzarella cheese	

- In a medium bowl stir together the crabmeat, cream cheese, garlic, mozzarella cheese, chives, and butter flavoring until well mixed.
- Serve as suggested.

Yield: 12 (2-tablespoon) servings

Calories: 30 (0% fat); Total Fat: 0 gm; Cholesterol: 15 mg; Carbohydrate: 1 gm; Dietary Fiber: 0 gm; Protein: 5 gm; Sodium: 122 mg
Diabetic Exchanges: 1 very lean meat

Preparation time: 15 minutes or less

Menu Ideas: As appetizers, have this with seafood-based entrées. Good entrée recommendations are Sautéed Scallops with Garlic with only 3 carbohydrates (page 180) and Seafood Stew (page 128), both from *Busy People's Diabetic Cookbook.* To complete the meal, serve with the Red Wine Vinaigrette Cucumber Salad (page 49) from *Down-Home Cooking Without the Down-Home Fat.* It has only 5 carbohydrates.

Chipped Beef & Cream Cheese Spread

The flavor combination of chipped beef and cream cheese with a kick of horseradish has just the right amount of pizzazz.

8 ounces fat-free cream cheese, softened	1 tablespoon horseradish sauce
2 teaspoons ranch salad dressing mix (do not make as directed)	1 (2.5-ounce) package chipped beef, finely chopped
1/4 cup fat-free sour cream	1 medium celery stalk, finely chopped (about 1/4 cup)
1 teaspoon dried chives or 2 teaspoons chopped fresh chives	

- In a medium bowl mix the cream cheese, salad dressing mix, and sour cream together until well blended.
- Stir in the chives, horseradish sauce, chipped beef, and celery until well mixed.
- Serve as suggested in menu ideas below.

Yield: 12 (1-tablespoon) servings

Calories: 37 (0% fat); Total Fat: 0 gm; Cholesterol: 8 mg; Carbohydrate: 3 gm; Dietary Fiber: 0 gm; Protein: 4 gm; Sodium: 257 mg
Diabetic Exchanges: 1/2 very lean meat

Preparation time: 15 minutes or less

Menu Ideas: For an appetizer or snack, it's terrific stuffed in celery or on low-carb crackers. For a light lunch, spread on half of a low-carb bagel or on low-carb, high-fiber toast and have Butter Rum Spiced Cider (with only 5 carbs) on page 61 in *Busy People's Diabetic Cookbook* on the side.

Horseradish & Bacon Cheese Spread

The teenagers went crazy over this. They were all surprised after they'd gobbled it all up to find out it had horseradish in it.

1 tablespoon horseradish	1 (8-ounce) package fat-free cream cheese, softened
1 tablespoon fat-free whipped salad dressing	
	1 tablespoon fat-free sour cream
1 teaspoon ranch salad dressing mix (do not make as directed)	3 tablespoons 30-percent-less-fat, real bacon bits (Hormel)
1 tablespoon dried parsley	

- In a medium bowl with a spatula, mix the horseradish, whipped salad dressing, ranch salad dressing mix, parsley, cream cheese, sour cream, and bacon bits together until smooth, creamy, and well blended.
- Keep chilled until ready to serve.

Yield: 8 (2-tablespoon) servings

Calories: 46 (14% fat); Total Fat: 1 gm; Cholesterol: 9 mg; Carbohydrate: 3 gm;
Dietary Fiber: 0 gm; Protein: 5 gm; Sodium: 275 mg
Diabetic Exchanges: 1 very lean meat

 Preparation time: 5 minutes or less

 Menu Idea: For an appetizer or snack, it's terrific stuffed in celery or in cherry tomatoes or on low-carb crackers. For a great snack or lunch spread on half of a low-carb bagel or on low-carb, high-fiber toast and have a Vanilla Steamer made with fat-free, low-carb milk for a beverage found on page 57 in *Busy People's Diabetic Cookbook.*

Salsa

Here's a great little salsa recipe for people who like to grow their own gardens.

1 large tomato, chopped (approximately 1²/₃ cups)	1 teaspoon ground cumin
¹/₄ cup chopped onion	1 medium green pepper, finely chopped (approximately 1¹/₄ cups)
¹/₂ cup chopped fresh cilantro	
1¹/₂ tablespoons minced garlic	Tabasco

- In a bowl stir the tomato, onion, cilantro, garlic, cumin, green pepper, and Tabasco to taste until well mixed.
- Cover and keep chilled until ready to eat.

Note: My husband likes salsa spicy, so he likes to add a 4-ounce can of diced chilies to the salsa as well. Me? I'm hot enough, thank you.

Yield: 32 (2-tablespoon) servings

Calories: 3 (0% fat); Total Fat: 0 gm; Cholesterol: 0 mg; Carbohydrate: 1 gm;
Dietary Fiber: 0 gm; Protein: 0 gm; Sodium: 1 mg
Diabetic Exchanges: Free

Preparation time: 20 minutes or less

Menu Idea: Great on low-carb tortilla chips or on Taco Lettuce Wraps on page 196 in this cookbook.

Garlic Butter

I loved the flavor and convenience of the pre-made garlic butter in the tubs at the specialty market. It was very expensive, though, so I came up with my own. This is every bit as delicious, a fraction of the cost, and has half the fat. This is absolutely fabulous. I love it.

4 teaspoons minced garlic (I use the kind in a jar.)	1 tablespoon dried parsley
¹/₂ cup light butter	¹/₂ teaspoon garlic salt

- In a small container microwave the minced garlic for 30 seconds, just enough to help release its full flavor.
- Add the butter, parsley, and garlic salt. Stir with a spatula until well blended.
- This does not need to be kept refrigerated; however, it is best to keep it covered.

Yield: 10 (1-tablespoon) servings

Calories: 42 (89% fat); Total Fat: 5 gm; Cholesterol: 16 mg; Carbohydrate: 0 gm; Dietary Fiber: 0 gm; Protein: 1 gm; Sodium: 105 mg
Diabetic Exchanges: 1 fat

Preparation time: 5 minutes or less

Menu Idea: I like to keep this on hand in a sealed container. It is wonderful for adding flavor to boring steamed vegetables. Simply stir a little into any vegetable dish after the vegetables have been fully cooked. This works with fresh, canned, or frozen veggies. It is also great on plain whole-grain toast to make garlic toast in a hurry.

Lemon-Herb Light Butter

Two thumbs up for this winning taste combination. It is slightly sweetened yet somewhat tart. It's a versatile spread that enhances the flavors of many foods. (See menu ideas below.)

1/2 cup reduced-fat, low-calorie butter or low-calorie margarine	1 teaspoon dried chives
1/8 teaspoon sugar-free lemonade drink mix (do not make as directed)	1 teaspoon dried parsley
	1 tablespoon minced garlic (I use the kind in a jar.)

- Mix the butter, lemonade drink mix, chives, parsley, and garlic together until well blended.
- Store in an airtight container.

Yield: 9 (1-tablespoon) servings

Calories: 46 (90% fat); Total Fat: 5 gm; Cholesterol: 18 mg; Carbohydrate: 0 gm; Dietary Fiber: 0 gm; Protein: 1 gm; Sodium: 63 mg
Diabetic Exchanges: 1 fat

Preparation time: 3 minutes or less

Menu Ideas: This spread is so versatile. Use on vegetables such as green beans or broccoli for a fantastic flavor boost. This is equally as tasty on brown rice or toasted whole grain, high-fiber bread for a unique taste experience that turns boring rice and bread into something extra special. It's also fantastic on steamed, baked, broiled, or grilled fish.

Clam Dip

This clam dip is versatile in its many uses and is good as an appetizer before any seafood-based meals.

¹/₄ teaspoon Old Bay seasoning, found in spice aisle	1 (16-ounce) container fat-free sour cream
1 teaspoon dried minced onion	2 tablespoons ranch salad dressing mix (do not make as directed)
¹/₂ cup fat-free shredded Cheddar cheese	
2 tablespoons fat-free whipped salad dressing	1 (10-ounce) can chopped clams, drained (reserve 1¹/₂ teaspoons juice)

- In a medium mixing bowl stir together the Old Bay, onion, cheese, whipped salad dressing, sour cream, ranch salad dressing mix, and clams until well mixed.
- Cover and keep refrigerated until ready to serve.

Yield: 24 (2-tablespoon) servings

Calories: 39 (0% fat); Total Fat: 0 gm; Cholesterol: 3 mg; Carbohydrate: 5 gm; Dietary Fiber: 0 gm; Protein: 4 gm; Sodium: 250 mg
Diabetic Exchanges: ¹/₂ other carbohydrate, ¹/₂ very lean meat

 Preparation time: 10 minutes or less

 Menu Ideas: Serve with fresh celery sticks, carrot sticks, or with strips of fresh red, green, or orange bell peppers. This is also good on low-carb crackers. Put a small dab on top of slices of fresh cucumber.

Strawberry Fruit Dip

This delectable dip can be used in many ways. It is very diversified.

1 cup fresh strawberries, cleaned	1 cup fat-free dessert whipped topping
4 individual packets Splenda	

- Put the strawberries and Splenda in a blender. Turn the blender on lowest speed for 10 seconds. (You want to have little chunks of strawberries visible.)
- Gently stir the sweetened, processed strawberries in a bowl with the dessert topping.
- Serve chilled.

Yield: 10 (2-tablespoon) servings

Calories: 19 (0% fat); Total Fat: 0 gm; Cholesterol: 0 mg; Carbohydrate: 4 gm; Dietary Fiber: 0 gm; Protein: 0 gm; Sodium: 4 mg
Diabetic Exchanges: Free

Preparation time: 5 minutes or less

Menu Idea: It can be used as a dip for fruit or chicken strips or on top of a bowl of strawberries. If you'd like, you can make Fruit Casseroles on page 247 of this cookbook and substitute this topping for the topping in that recipe.

Cherry Cheesecake Dip

The rich, smooth, and creamy flavors we love in cherry cheesecakes are spotlighted in this dip.

1 cup frozen no-sugar-added tart cherries	$1/2$ teaspoon vanilla extract
4 ounces fat-free cream cheese	$2/3$ cup fat-free, low-carb milk
$1/2$ cup Splenda Granular, measures like sugar	

- Put the cherries, cream cheese, Splenda, vanilla extract, and milk in a blender.
- Cover and process on high for 2 to 3 minutes or until smooth and creamy.
- Pour into a serving dish. Serve with your favorite low-carb fruits such as strawberries.

Yield: 10 (2-tablespoon) servings

Calories: 29 (0% fat); Total Fat: 0 gm; Cholesterol: 2 mg; Carbohydrate: 4 gm; Dietary Fiber: 0 gm; Protein: 3 gm; Sodium: 70 mg
Diabetic Exchanges: $1/2$ very lean meat

Preparation time: 5 minutes or less

Menu Ideas: Serve this dip with your favorite low-carb fruits as a light dessert, snack, or as part of a buffet table for breakfast, lunch, or brunch. I suggest the Cream Cheese & Crab Frittata on page 171 with this for a complete meal.

Super Easy Soups & Salads

*Indicates a slow cooker recipe

Country Chicken Soup

Feel free to use as many of your homegrown, low-carb vegetables in this soup as you would like. The more the merrier.

I	**(49-ounce) can fat-free chicken broth**	2	**small zucchini, cut into bite-size pieces**
2	**(13-ounce) cans fat-free chicken breast, not drained**	2	**(14.5-ounce) cans stewed tomatoes with green pepper**
2	**tablespoons Mrs. Dash table seasoning blend**	I	**cup finely chopped celery (about 4 stalks)**
I	**cup chopped onion (fresh or frozen)**		

- Stir together in a large slow cooker the chicken broth, chicken, Mrs. Dash, onion, zucchini, tomatoes, and celery.
- Cover and cook on low for 4 to 5 hours.

Yield: 12 (1-cup) servings

Calories: 102 (11% fat); Total Fat: 1 gm; Cholesterol: 26 mg; Carbohydrate: 8 gm; Dietary Fiber: 2 gm; Protein: 14 gm; Sodium: 694 mg
Diabetic Exchanges: 1½ vegetable, 1½ very lean meat

Preparation time: 7 minutes or less

Menu Idea: For dessert have from the *Busy People's Diabetic Cookbook* either Citrus Spice Cookies (with 6 carbs) on page 240 or Very Vanilla Cookies (with 7 carbs) on page 239.

Chicken Olé Soup

This has the southwestern flavors we like without a lot of the calories or carbs.

2	(14.5-ounce) cans stewed tomatoes with green peppers	5	(10-ounce) cans chicken
1/2	cup chunky salsa	1	(10-ounce) bag frozen chopped broccoli
1	(4-ounce) can green chilies	1/2	teaspoon ground cumin
3	(14-ounce) cans fat-free, reduced-sodium chicken broth		

- In a slow cooker stir together the tomatoes, salsa, green chilies, chicken broth, chicken, broccoli, and cumin until well mixed.
- Cover and cook on low for 4 hours.

Yield: 17 (1-cup) servings

Calories: 113 (14% fat); Total Fat: 2 gm; Cholesterol: 35 mg; Carbohydrate: 5 gm; Dietary Fiber: 2 gm; Protein: 17 gm; Sodium: 681 mg
Diabetic Exchanges: 1 vegetable, 2 lean meat

Preparation time: 10 minutes

Menu Idea: The Sour Cream Drop Biscuits on page 50 are a fine choice with this soup.

Chicken, Broccoli & Mushroom Soup

This is a very mild-flavored soup. You may want to add salt and pepper once it is fully cooked; however, I did not to keep the sodium low.

1	(16-ounce) package sliced fresh mushrooms	2	(15-ounce) cans fat-free, low-sodium chicken broth
1	(16-ounce) bags frozen broccoli pieces	2	(13-ounce) cans fat-free chicken breast (do not drain)
1	cup frozen chopped onion	2	tablespoons Worcestershire sauce
2	tablespoons minced garlic (from a jar)		

- Stir together in a large slow cooker the mushrooms, broccoli, onion, garlic, chicken broth, chicken, and Worcestershire sauce until well mixed.
- Cover and cook on low for 6 to 8 hours.

Yield: 16 (1-cup) servings

Calories: 72 (13% fat); Total Fat: 1 gm; Cholesterol: 21 mg; Carbohydrate: 4 gm; Dietary Fiber: 2 gm; Protein: 12 gm; Sodium: 143 mg
Diabetic Exchanges: 1 vegetable, 1½ very lean meat

Preparation time: 7 minutes or less

Menu Idea: Since this soup is so mild, I served it with a zesty and crunchy side dish of Nacho Cucumber Slices on page 155 of this book.

Spicy Chicken & Vegetables Soup

This is so full of robust flavor, you'll forget it is low-carb.

1 **(49-ounce) can chicken fat-free broth**	2 **medium zucchini, cut into ¹/₄-inch slices**
1 **(16-ounce) jar salsa**	1 **red bell pepper, chopped (about 1 cup)**
1 **pound bag frozen broccoli, cauliflower, and carrot blend**	
2 **(13-ounce) cans fat-free chicken breast**	2 **(14.5-ounce) cans diced tomatoes with green chilies**

- Spray a large slow cooker with nonfat cooking spray.
- In the slow cooker put the chicken broth, salsa, frozen vegetables, chicken, zucchini, bell pepper, and diced tomatoes.
- Cover and cook on low for 6 to 8 hours.

Yield: 18 (1-cup) servings

Calories: 75 (12% fat); Total Fat: 1 gm; Cholesterol: 17 mg; Carbohydrate: 5 gm;
Dietary Fiber: 2 gm; Protein: 10 gm; Sodium: 617 mg
Diabetic Exchanges: 1 vegetable, 1 very lean meat

Preparation time: 7 minutes or less

 **Menu Idea:** *Busy People's Diabetic Cookbook* has many high-quality, low-carb cookies to satisfy your sweet-tooth after this festive soup, such as Double Chocolate Graham Cookies (with 5 carbs) on page 244, Sugar-Free Lemon Meringue Cookies (with only 1 carb) on page 243, and Soft Apple Cinnamon Cookies (with 7 carbs) on page 236.

Crab & Asparagus Soup

Light, smooth, and just right for rainy days when you want soothing comfort food without a lot of calories.

3 cups low-carb milk	3 (6-ounce) cans real crabmeat, not drained
3 teaspoons whole wheat flour	
1 cup shredded fat-free Cheddar cheese	1 (14.5-ounce) can asparagus pieces, drained

- In a blender mix the milk, flour, and cheese on medium speed for 30 seconds.
- Pour into a nonstick, medium-size saucepan.
- Add the crabmeat and asparagus.
- Heat about 10 minutes on medium heat, stirring frequently.
- Once the mixture comes to a low boil, remove it from the heat. If time permits, it is best to let the soup sit for about 4 to 5 minutes before serving. Soup will thicken as it cools.

Yield: 7 (1-cup) servings

Calories: 140 (9% fat); Total Fat: 1 gm; Cholesterol: 70 mg; Carbohydrate: 4 gm; Dietary Fiber: 0 gm; Protein: 27 gm; Sodium: 656 mg
Diabetic Exchanges: $\frac{1}{2}$ skim milk, 3 very lean meat

Preparation time: 5 minutes
Cooking time: 10 minutes
Total time: 15 minutes

Menu Idea: Put a few low-fat oyster crackers on top of each serving. Then sprinkle lightly with parsley, if desired, for an enhanced appearance. The Fancy-Shmancy Salad (page 112 in this book) and a couple of Orange Sugar Cookies (page 231) with only 7 carbs found in *Busy People's Diabetic Cookbook* make a nice luncheon or light dinner.

Egg Drop Soup

Brenda Crosser sent in this recipe, stating it was quite tasty. I must agree.

4 cups fat-free chicken broth	¹/₄ cup liquid egg substitute
¹/₂ cup sliced mushrooms	2 tablespoons cornstarch
2 cups chopped bean sprouts	¹/₄ cup water

- Bring the chicken broth, mushrooms, and bean sprouts to a boil in a large saucepan over high heat.
- Slowly add the egg substitute to the boiling broth, stirring constantly.
- Mix the cornstarch and water together in a cup until the cornstarch is completely dissolved and then add the mixture to the boiling broth slowly.
- Stir as the soup thickens, about 10 minutes.
- Serve hot.

Yield: 6 (1-cup) servings

Calories: 38 (0% fat); Total Fat: 0 gm; Cholesterol: 0 mg; Carbohydrate: 6 gm; Dietary Fiber: 1 gm; Protein: 4 gm; Sodium: 281 mg
Diabetic Exchanges: 1 vegetable

Preparation time: 10 minutes or less
Cooking time: 20 minutes or less
Total time: 30 minutes or less

Menu Idea: Start oriental-themed entrées with this soup, such as the Garlic Beef on page 211 in *Busy People's Diabetic Cookbook*.

Zesty Soup

This reminds me of minestrone soup without any beans or pasta.

1 pound ground eye of round	2 teaspoons Mrs. Dash's basil and tomato seasoning blend
1 cup chopped onion	1 (12-ounce) bag sausage-flavored Ground Meatless* (I use Morningstar Farms)
1 cup chopped green bell pepper	
1 (46-ounce) can low-sodium tomato juice	1 individual packet Splenda

- In a large soup pan brown the beef with the onion until fully cooked.
- Add the green pepper, tomato juice, Mrs. Dash's seasoning, and sausage. Bring to a low boil; this will take about 10 minutes.
- Let simmer 5 minutes. Stir in the Splenda once the heat is off.
- Serve hot.

Note: Ground Meatless is a vegetarian meat substitute made by Morningstar Farms. It's found in the freezer section of your grocery store. If desired, you can use cooked and crumbled turkey Italian sausage instead, but the nutritional information will be different.

Yield: 8 (1-cup) servings

Calories: 157 (16% fat); Total Fat: 3 gm; Cholesterol: 29 mg; Carbohydrate: 13 gm; Dietary Fiber: 3 gm; Protein: 21 gm; Sodium: 197 mg
Diabetic Exchanges: 3 vegetable, 2½ very lean meat

Preparation time: 5 minutes
Cooking time: 20 minutes
Total time: 25 minutes

Menu Idea: Have an Italian-themed, soup-and-salad dinner or luncheon by serving the Little Italy Tossed Salad on page 120 in this book.

Southwestern Chicken Chili

This spicy flavor will wake you up and warm you down to your bones. It's just the satisfying answer for a chilly day.

5	(13-ounce) cans fat-free chicken breast, not drained	1	(4-ounce) can green chilies, chopped
2	(14.5-ounce) cans diced tomatoes with onion and green pepper	1	(16-ounce) jar mild salsa
1	(49-ounce) can fat-free, low-sodium chicken broth	2	teaspoons chili powder

- Spray a slow cooker with nonfat cooking spray.
- In the prepared slow cooker pour 2 cans of chicken with the juice. With a fork shred the chicken.
- Add to the slow cooker the remaining 3 cans of chicken, allowing these cans of chicken pieces to remain as chunks.
- Then add and stir in the tomatoes, chicken broth, chilies, salsa, and chili powder until well mixed with the chicken.
- Cover and cook on low for 5 to 7 hours.

Yield: 18 (1-cup) servings

Calories: 140 (14% fat); Total Fat: 2 gm; Cholesterol: 46 mg; Carbohydrate: 5 gm; Dietary Fiber: 1 gm; Protein: 23 gm; Sodium: 504 mg
Diabetic Exchanges: 1 vegetable, 3 very lean meat

Preparation time: 5 minutes

Menu Idea: Because this soup doesn't have any crunch to it, I like having the Nacho Cucumber Slices on page 155 of this book with this soup for added crunch and texture to the meal.

Beef & Cabbage Soup

Everyone agreed; the flavor of this is really good. It sticks to your ribs but not your hips or thighs.

1	pound ground eye of round	1	(14.5-ounce) can stewed tomatoes
1	(16-ounce) bag coleslaw mix	1	teaspoon Mrs. Dash table blend seasoning
1/4	cup chopped frozen onion		
2	(14-ounce) cans fat-free beef broth	2	tablespoons Worcestershire sauce

- In a large soup pan or Dutch oven cook the beef over medium-high heat until brown. Drain, rinse, and discard any juices.
- Add the coleslaw mix, onion, beef broth, stewed tomatoes, Mrs. Dash, and Worcestershire sauce. Bring to a low boil over medium heat.
- Cover and let simmer for 10 minutes, stirring occasionally.

Yield: 9 servings

Calories: 109 (21% fat); Total Fat: 3 gm; Cholesterol: 28 mg; Carbohydrate: 7 gm; Dietary Fiber: 2 gm; Protein: 14 gm; Sodium: 249 mg
Diabetic Exchanges: 1½ vegetable, 1½ lean meat

Preparation time: 5 minutes
Cooking time: 15 minutes
Total time: 20 minutes or less

Menu Idea: This is great on a cold night or after a brisk walk in the chilly outdoors. Add some fat-free, whole wheat crackers and my Cheese Ball recipe (with only 6 carbs per serving) on page 20 in *Busy People's Down-Home Cooking Without the Down-Home Fat.*

Cheddar Seafood Bisque

Because this is expensive to make, I save this for extra special occasions.

3	cups low-carb milk	I	(6-ounce) can real shrimp, not drained
2	cups fat-free Cheddar cheese		
3	teaspoons whole wheat flour	I	(6-ounce) can real crabmeat, not drained
I	(6-ounce) can real lobster, not drained		

- In a large saucepan blend the milk, cheese, and flour until smooth.
- Place the saucepan over medium heat and add the lobster, shrimp, and crabmeat.
- Heat for 12 to 15 minutes while stirring frequently. Serve hot in a bowl.

Yield: 5 (1-cup) servings

Calories: 218 (6% fat); Total Fat: 1 gm; Cholesterol: 124 mg; Carbohydrate: 5 gm; Dietary Fiber: 0 gm; Protein: 44 gm; Sodium: 858 mg
Diabetic Exchanges: $\frac{1}{2}$ skim milk, 5 very lean meat

Preparation time: 5 minutes
Cooking time: 12 to 15 minutes
Total time: 20 minutes

Menu Idea: For an expensive, five-course meal, serve this with the Fancy-Shmancy Salad (page 112), Confetti Topped Asparagus (page 157), Grilled & Lightly Barbequed Shrimp Kebobs (page 168), and Very Cherry Soft Sorbet (page 233) all in this book.

Chicken & Seafood Stew

This hearty stew is a unique and delicious flavor combination that is as tasty as it is original. I really like the two flavors together and think they actually complement each other.

1	pound skinless, boneless chicken breast, cut into bite-size pieces	1	(6-ounce) can shrimp, do not drain
1	cup fat-free, reduced-sodium chicken broth	1	(6-ounce) can real crabmeat, do not drain
1½	tablespoons cornstarch		
½	teaspoon Old Bay seasoning (found in spice section)		

- Spray a large 12-inch, nonstick skillet with nonfat cooking spray.
- Cook the chicken over medium-high heat, covered, for 2 to 3 minutes. Turn the chicken over and continue cooking until golden on both sides.
- While the chicken is cooking, stir together in a bowl the chicken broth, cornstarch, and seasoning until the cornstarch is completely dissolved.
- When done, transfer the cooked chicken to a covered dish to keep warm. Reduce the heat to medium and add the chicken broth mixture to the skillet. Cook, stirring constantly, until the broth becomes thick.
- Stir in the shrimp and crabmeat. Add the cooked chicken.
- Cover, reduce the heat to low, and cook on low for 2 to 3 minutes or until fully heated. Serve hot.

Yield: 4 (1-cup) servings

Calories: 234 (12% fat); Total Fat: 3 gm; Cholesterol: 177 mg; Carbohydrate: 3 gm; Dietary Fiber: 0 gm; Protein: 45 gm; Sodium: 464 mg
Diabetic Exchanges: 6 very lean meat

Preparation time: 6 minutes
Cooking time: 9 minutes
Total time: 15 minutes or less

Menu Idea: I recommend serving this with French-Style Simmered Green Beans (with only 6 carbs) on page 170 or the Seasoned Buttered Broccoli (with only 5 carbs) on page 172 both in *Busy People's Diabetic Cookbook*.

Venison Stew

I'm amazed at how the turnips ended up tasting like slow-roasted potatoes in this hearty stew that men especially enjoy.

2	pounds venison, cut into bite-size pieces	2	turnips, peeled and diced
2	(14.5-ounce) cans stewed tomatoes with onions and green peppers	1/2	teaspoon dried thyme
		4	medium onions, peeled and cut into 8 wedges each
1	(16-ounce) bag frozen sliced carrots	1	(12-ounce) jar fat-free beef gravy

- Spray a slow cooker with nonfat cooking spray.
- In the slow cooker stir together the venison, tomatoes, carrots, turnips, thyme, onions, and gravy until well mixed.
- Cover and cook on low for 10 to 12 hours.

Note: You can also substitute an eye of round roast for the venison if desired.

Yield: 15 (1-cup) servings

Calories: 129 (11% fat); Total Fat: 2 gm; Cholesterol: 53 mg; Carbohydrate: 13 gm; Dietary Fiber: 2 gm; Protein: 15 gm; Sodium: 390 mg
Diabetic Exchanges: 2$\frac{1}{2}$ vegetable, 2 very lean meat

Preparation time: 15 minutes

Menu Idea: Round this hearty stew off with a freshly tossed Red Lettuce Salad on page 113 of this book.

Spicy Bean-less Chili

Just right for when you want the flavors of chili without the heaviness of chili. My daughters' friends gobbled this up so fast, there wasn't any left for my husband or me. They loved how spicy it was.

1 pound Ground Meatless* or 1 pound ground eye of round	1 (15-ounce) can fat-free beef broth
1/2 cup chopped onion (fresh or frozen)	1 teaspoon chili powder
2 tablespoons minced garlic	1 teaspoon ground cumin
2 (14-ounce) cans stewed tomatoes with green chilies	

- In a large, nonstick soup pan add the Ground Meatless, onion, garlic, stewed tomatoes, beef broth, chili powder, and cumin.
- Cook over medium-low heat until it comes to a low boil and boil for 5 minutes.
- Serve hot.

Note: Ground Meatless is a vegetarian meat substitute made by Morningstar Farms. If using ground eye of round, cook it and drain all the fat before mixing it with the vegetables and spices.

Yield: 5 (1-cup) servings

(with Ground Meatless) Calories: 133 (0% fat); Total Fat: 0 gm; Cholesterol: 0 mg; Carbohydrate: 16 gm; Dietary Fiber: 6 gm; Protein: 18 gm; Sodium: 939 mg
Diabetic Exchanges: 1/2 starch, 2 vegetable, 2 very lean meat
(with ground eye of round) Calories: 168 (25% fat); Total Fat: 5 gm; Cholesterol: 50 mg; Carbohydrate: 10 gm; Dietary Fiber: 2 gm; Protein: 23 gm; Sodium: 769 mg
Diabetic Exchanges: 2 vegetable, 2 1/2 lean meat

Preparation time: 10 minutes or less
Cooking time: 10 minutes
Total time: 20 minutes or less

Menu Idea: I recommend a side dish you don't need to watch over, such as nachos made in the microwave with low-carbohydrate tortilla chips and reduced-fat or fat-free cheddar cheese.

Country-Style Beef Vegetable Soup

This was a huge hit at our home for dinner. Everyone asked for seconds. That is saying a lot, especially for a vegetable soup assembled in less than five minutes. My husband really liked the chunks of beef.

1 (14.5-ounce) can fat-free, low-sodium beef broth	1 cup chopped celery
3 (12-ounce) cans beef	1 teaspoon Mrs. Dash table blend seasoning
1 pound coleslaw mix	1 (16-ounce) jar mild salsa
1 (14.5-ounce) can green beans	

- Put the beef broth, beef, coleslaw, green beans, celery, Mrs. Dash, and salsa in a slow cooker and stir until well mixed.
- Cover and cook on low for 4 hours.

Yield: 12 (1-cup) servings

Calories: 112 (15% fat); Total Fat: 2 gm; Cholesterol: 39 mg; Carbohydrate: 6 gm; Dietary Fiber: 1 gm; Protein: 16 gm; Sodium: 768 mg
Diabetic Exchanges: 1 vegetable, 2 very lean meat

Preparation time: 5 minutes or less

Menu Idea: If you want to complete your meal with something a little sweet, try one of the many wonderful low-carb cookie recipes in *Busy People's Diabetic Cookbook,* such as Soft Apple Cinnamon Cookies (with only 7 carbs) on page 236 or the Double Chocolate Graham Cookies (with only 5 carbs) on page 244.

Italian Stew

This is one of my all-time favorite stew recipes.

1 **(12-ounce) bag sausage-flavored Ground Meatless***	1 **cup frozen chopped onion**
4 **small zucchini, cut into 1/2-inch slices (about 8 cups)**	1 **(15-ounce) can fat-free, low-sodium beef broth**
3 **(14.5-ounce) cans Italian-style stewed tomatoes**	1 **teaspoon Italian seasoning blend**

- In a slow cooker mix together the sausage, zucchini, stewed tomatoes, onion, broth, and seasoning blend.
- Cover and cook on low for 5 to 6 hours or on high for 2 hours.

*Note: Ground Meatless is a vegetarian meat substitute made by Morningstar Farms. It's found in the freezer section of your grocery store. If desired, you can use cooked and crumbled turkey Italian sausage instead, but the nutritional information will be different.

Yield: 13 (1-cup) servings

Calories: 81 (17% fat); Total Fat: 2 gm; Cholesterol: 0 mg; Carbohydrate: 10 gm; Dietary Fiber: 3 gm; Protein: 7 gm; Sodium: 399 mg
Diabetic Exchanges: 2 vegetable, ½ lean meat

Preparation time: 10 minutes or less

Menu Idea: Complete this meal with a fresh garden salad topped with my homemade Buttermilk Ranch Salad Dressing on page 53 in Busy People's Low-Fat Cookbook and the Pinwheel Dinner Rolls on page 64 of the same cookbook.

Slow-Roasted Beef & Bell Peppers Stew

This has a very good flavor and reminds me a lot of a steak and bell pepper stir-fry. However, the peppers in this recipe are not crisp; they are fully cooked.

2	tablespoons light soy sauce	6	small onions, quartered
2	pounds eye of round, cut into strips (about 2 x ¼ inches)	1	(5.5-ounce) can crushed pineapple, not drained
2	large green bell peppers, cut into strips	1	tablespoon Worcestershire sauce
2	large red bell peppers, cut into strips		

- Spray a large slow cooker with nonfat cooking spray.
- Layer in the prepared slow cooker from the bottom in this order: soy sauce, beef strips, green bell pepper strips, red bell pepper strips, quartered onions, pineapple with its juice, and Worcestershire sauce.
- Cover and cook on low for 6 to 7 hours.

Yield: 12 (1-cup) servings

Calories: 138 (18% fat); Total Fat: 3 gm; Cholesterol: 39 mg; Carbohydrate: 10 gm; Dietary Fiber: 2 gm; Protein: 18 gm; Sodium: 153 mg
Diabetic Exchanges: 2 vegetable, 2 lean meat

Preparation time: 30 minutes or less

Menu Idea: As a refreshing beverage, Mint Tea (page 25) with only 1 little carbohydrate complements the flavors of this entrée, as does the Marshmallow Applesauce Dessert (page 200) with only 12 carbohydrates, both from *Busy People's Slow Cooker Cookbook.*

Sausage & Tomato Chowder

My friends were crazy about this robust soup. I wish you could have seen how excited they were. They simply could not believe this was vegetarian or low-carb because it is so full-bodied and hearty.

1 (12-ounce) package frozen sausage-flavored Ground Meatless* or 1-pound Italian turkey sausage, cooked, rinsed, drained, and crumbled	2 (15-ounce) cans fat-free, low-sodium beef broth
2 (14.5-ounce) cans Italian-style stewed tomatoes	1 (16-ounce) package sliced fresh mushrooms
	1 cup chopped onion (fresh or frozen)

- Stir together in a large slow cooker the sausage, tomatoes, beef broth, mushrooms, and onion.
- Cover and cook on low for 4½ to 6 hours.

Note: Ground Meatless is a vegetarian meat substitute made by Morningstar Farms. It tastes just as good, but without all the fat. It's found in the freezer section of your grocery store.

Yield: 11 (1-cup) servings

(with Ground Meatless) Calories: 97 (17% fat); Total Fat: 2 gm; Cholesterol: 0 mg; Carbohydrate: 11 gm; Dietary Fiber: 3 gm; Protein: 10 gm; Sodium: 426 mg
Diabetic Exchanges: 2 vegetable, 1 lean meat
(with turkey sausage) Calories: 112 (35% fat); Total Fat: 4 gm; Cholesterol: 35 mg; Carbohydrate: 8 gm; Dietary Fiber: 2 gm; Protein: 9 gm; Sodium: 511 mg
Diabetic Exchanges: 1½ vegetable, 1 lean meat

 Preparation time: 7 minutes or less

 Menu Idea: A simple side salad such as the Red Lettuce Salad on page 113 is all you need for a well-balanced, healthy, low-carb meal.

Savory Beef Stew

My husband had a good idea for people who want to add extra carbs. He had his stew over toast and loved it. Me? I didn't even miss the potatoes or carrots in this low-carb stew, because this gravy is so rich, smooth, and satisfying.

1 pound lean beef stew meat, cut into bite-size pieces	1 (15-ounce) jar pearl onions
1 (14.5-ounce) can stewed tomatoes with onions and green peppers	2 celery stalks, cut into 1-inch pieces
	1/2 teaspoon dried thyme
1 (8-ounce) package sliced fresh mushrooms	1 (12-ounce) jar fat-free beef gravy

- Spray a slow cooker with nonfat cooking spray.
- Stir together in the prepared slow cooker the meat, tomatoes, mushrooms, onions, celery, thyme, and gravy until well mixed.
- Cover and cook on low for 4 to 6 hours.

Yield: 6½ (1-cup) servings

Calories: 176 (32% fat); Total Fat: 6 gm; Cholesterol: 48 mg; Carbohydrate: 13 gm; Dietary Fiber: 2 gm; Protein: 17 gm; Sodium: 579 mg
Diabetic Exchanges: 3 vegetable, 2 lean meat

Preparation time: 5 minutes

Menu Idea: I serve the Bran Muffin Bites (page 51) from this cookbook and the Red Wine Vinaigrette Cucumber Salad (page 49) from *Busy People's Down-Home Cooking Without the Down-Home Fat* for a comforting and satisfying dinner.

Bibb Lettuce Salad with Pear & Feta Cheese

This is one of those super-fast-to-put-together salads that impress people because of its excellent flavor combination of ingredients and beautiful appearance.

1 head leafy green lettuce, cleaned and torn into bite-size pieces (about 6 cups)	1 tablespoon plus 1 teaspoon walnuts, finely chopped
1/2 pear, cut into tiny pieces (about 1/2 cup chopped)	4 strawberries, thinly sliced
2 tablespoons reduced-fat feta cheese	1/2 cup fat-free red wine vinaigrette salad dressing

For each salad:

- Place 1 1/2 cups lettuce in each salad bowl.
- Top with 1/8 cup chopped pear, 1/2 tablespoon feta cheese, 1 teaspoon walnuts, and 1 strawberry.
- Cover and keep chilled until ready to eat.
- Drizzle 2 tablespoons salad dressing on top right before serving.
- Repeat this procedure with the remaining ingredients.

Yield: 4 (1 1/2-cup) servings

Calories: 70 (30% fat); Total Fat: 2 gm; Cholesterol: 2 mg; Carbohydrate: 10 gm; Dietary Fiber: 2 gm; Protein: 2 gm; Sodium: 492 mg
Diabetic Exchanges: 1/2 fruit, 1/2 fat

Preparation time: 15 minutes or less

Menu Idea: This salad especially complements the Pork Tenderloin recipe (with only 10 carbs) on page 172 in *Busy People's Slow Cooker Cookbook.*

Fresh Lettuce Salad

Make a huge green salad once a week to last throughout the entire week. Store it in Ziploc bags with all the air squeezed out to save space in the refrigerator. When ready to eat, simply garnish as desired.

1 medium head romaine lettuce, chopped (about 7 cups)	1 medium head red leaf lettuce, chopped (about 7 cups)
1 medium head green leaf lettuce, chopped (about 7 cups)	1 (10-ounce) bag washed baby spinach

- Rinse the romaine, green leaf lettuce, red leaf lettuce, and the spinach leaves with water.
- Cut the lettuce with a stainless steel butcher knife (or tear them into bite-size pieces). Hold the entire head of lettuce tightly together. Cut off the core and discard. Cut into ½-inch slices, turn the leaves and cut again until you have bite-size pieces.
- Toss all of the leaves together in a very large bowl.
- Keep in an airtight container or in Ziploc bags with all of the air squeezed out.

Yield: 14 (2-cup) servings

Calories: 16 (0% fat); Total Fat: 0 gm; Cholesterol: 0 mg; Carbohydrate: 3 gm; Dietary Fiber: 1 gm; Protein: 1 gm; Sodium: 29 mg
Diabetic Exchanges: Free

Preparation time: 20 minutes

 **Menu Idea:** Instead of buying prepackaged, precut lettuce use this to make the Water Chestnut Salad on page 136, Little Italy Tossed Salad on page 120, and the Taco Salad on page 122, all in this book.

Spinach Salad with Warm Sweet & Sour Dressing

Two thumbs up for this delicious warm salad dressing. It makes the salad. If you'd like, you can substitute other types of lettuce for the spinach.

3	tablespoons 30% less fat, real bacon bits	2	(10-ounce) bags fresh baby spinach leaves, cleaned
1/4	cup apple cider vinegar	2	tablespoons grated Parmesan cheese
2	individual packets Splenda		
1/4	teaspoon garlic salt		
I	(15-ounce) can diced tomatoes, drained		

- In a nonstick saucepan bring the bacon pieces, vinegar, Splenda, garlic salt, and tomatoes to a boil stirring occasionally. This will take about 4 minutes. As soon as it comes to a low boil, remove from the heat. Let cool for a minute or two.
- Put the spinach in a large salad bowl.
- Toss the spinach with the warm dressing. Sprinkle with the cheese. The spinach may wilt a little.

Yield: 6 (1½-cup) servings

Calories: 58 (21% fat); Total Fat: 2 gm; Cholesterol: 6 mg; Carbohydrate: 8 gm; Dietary Fiber: 3 gm; Protein: 5 gm; Sodium: 320 mg
Diabetic Exchanges: 1½ vegetable, ½ fat

Preparation time: 5 minutes or less
Cooking time: 5 minutes or less
Total time: 10 minutes or less

Menu Idea: This salad, with its slight tangy flavor, will add zip to a dinner of Steak on a Stick (page 120) with only 1 carb in *Busy People's Down-Home Cooking Without the Down-Home Fat* and Asparagus & Mushrooms (page 70) with only 6 carbs in that same cookbook.

Marinated Fresh Vegetable Garden Salad

This salad is a perfect way to use a wide assortment of your fresh, homegrown vegetables straight from the garden.

$3/4$ cup water	1 large cucumber, sliced (about 3 cups)
$1/3$ cup Splenda Granular, measures like sugar	1 red bell pepper, chopped (about 1 cup)
$3/4$ cup fat-free red wine vinaigrette salad dressing	2 green onions, chopped (about $1/4$ cup)
1 head fresh broccoli florets (about 3 cups broccoli tops)	

- In a 1-gallon Ziploc bag put the water, Splenda, and salad dressing. Seal the bag. Shake until the dressing is well blended.
- Put the broccoli tops, cucumber, red bell pepper, and green onions in the bag with the prepared dressing. Let them marinate 15 minutes. Actually the salad tastes fine not marinated; however, I think it tastes best after the vegetables have had an opportunity to rest in the marinade a while.
- Seal and keep refrigerated until ready to eat.

Yield: 14 ($1/2$-cup) servings

Calories: 20 (0% fat); Total Fat: 0 gm; Cholesterol: 0 mg; Carbohydrate: 4 gm; Dietary Fiber: 1 gm; Protein: 1 gm; Sodium: 182 mg
Diabetic Exchanges: Free

Preparation time: 15 minutes or less
Marinating time: 15 minutes
Total time: 30 minutes or less

Menu Ideas: This is grand with picnic-style foods, especially because all of the vegetables are fresh and in season for Midwesterners and northern folks during the picnic seasons. Lean grilled hamburgers, steak, pork tenderloin, fish, chicken, or fat-free hot dogs all go well with this salad.

Crabby Garden Salad with Sweet & Spicy Bacon-Cheddar Dressing

Don't let the grouchy recipe title turn you away from this wonderful salad. You are going to really like this flavor combination. It is so good.

1 tablespoon distilled vinegar	1 tablespoon 30 percent less fat, real bacon pieces (Hormel)
2 tablespoons picante sauce	
1 individual packet Splenda	2 tablespoons shredded fat-free Cheddar cheese
4 cups red leaf lettuce (about 1/3 head)	1/2 cup crabmeat

- In bowl stir together the vinegar, picante sauce, and Splenda until well mixed.
- Gently toss the lettuce, bacon, cheese, and crabmeat together in the dressing.
- Serve immediately.

Yield: 2 (2-cup) servings

Calories: 91 (25% fat); Total Fat: 3 gm; Cholesterol: 34 mg; Carbohydrate: 8 gm; Dietary Fiber: 3 gm; Protein: 11 gm; Sodium: 421 mg
Diabetic Exchanges: 1½ vegetable, 1 lean meat

Yield: 1 (4-cup) servings

Calories: 183 (25% fat); Total Fat: 5 gm; Cholesterol: 68 mg; Carbohydrate: 15 gm; Dietary Fiber: 5 gm; Protein: 21 gm; Sodium: 843 mg
Diabetic Exchanges: 3 vegetable, 2 lean meat

 **Preparation time:** 5 minutes or less

Menu Idea: For a meal in itself eat this with a few low-carb crackers. As a side salad, serve this with fish or seafood-based recipes such as Sautéed Scallops with Garlic (with only 3 carbs) on page 180 in *Busy People's Diabetic Cookbook* or the Creamy Shrimp & Bacon with Mushrooms Dinner (with 11 carbs) on page 184 also in *the Busy People's Diabetic Cookbook.*

Feta & Basil-Topped Tomatoes with Red Wine Vinaigrette Salad Dressing

Not only does this terrific recipe taste fresh, cool, and flavorful, it's also very pretty.

1 large fresh tomato, sliced into 6 slices	1/4 cup chopped green onion tops
1/4 cup fat-free red wine vinaigrette salad dressing	1 teaspoon dried basil or 2 teaspoons finely chopped fresh basil
1/3 cup crumbled reduced-fat feta cheese	

- Arrange the tomato slices on a serving plate with a ½-inch edge so the dressing will not run off.
- Drizzle the dressing over the tomato slices.
- In a small bowl stir together the feta, green onions, and basil until well mixed, yet still crumbly.
- Sprinkle the cheese mixture over the tomatoes, approximately 2 teaspoons on each slice.
- Serve as is, or cover and keep refrigerated until ready to eat.

Yield: 3 (2-slice) servings

Calories: 55 (31% fat); Total Fat: 2 gm; Cholesterol: 6 mg; Carbohydrate: 6 gm; Dietary Fiber: 1 gm; Protein: 4 gm; Sodium: 498 mg
Diabetic Exchanges: 1 vegetable

Preparation time: 5 minutes or less

Menu Idea: Serve with simple entrées such as Pork Tenderloin with only 10 carbohydrates on page 172 in *Busy People's Slow Cooker Cookbook* or Chicken with Cool & Creamy Lime Sauce (with only 9 carbs) on page 212 in *Busy People's Diabetic Cookbook*.

Cucumber, Dill & Tomato Salad

This salad is ready to eat once ingredients are stirred together; however, I think the flavor is improved when it has time to rest and let the sour cream incorporate the flavors of the seasonings.

1/2 teaspoon dried dill	1 pint grape tomatoes*
1/2 cup fat-free sour cream	1 medium cucumber, cut into thin slices
1/2 teaspoon dried basil	
Dash of lite salt (optional)	

- In a medium-size mixing bowl stir together the dill, sour cream, basil, and salt (optional) until well blended.
- Gently stir in the tomatoes and cucumbers, making sure all of the vegetables are coated with the dressing.
- Cover and keep chilled until ready to eat.

Note: Cherry tomatoes can be substituted: however, the grape tomatoes tend to be sweeter.

Yield: 7 (½-cup) servings

Calories: 41 (0% fat); Total Fat: 0 gm; Cholesterol: 3 mg; Carbohydrate: 8 gm; Dietary Fiber: 1 gm; Protein: 2 gm; Sodium: 20 mg
Diabetic Exchanges: 1½ vegetable

Preparation time: 15 minutes or less

Menu Idea: This salad tastes good with the Garlic Parmesan Chicken on page 185 of this book or any home-style entrée.

Fancy-Shmancy Salad

Presentation is the name of the game in this recipe. Since each salad has to be made separately, I am giving the directions for one salad, and, of course, you can simply multiply the recipe for however many servings you need.

5	medium romaine lettuce leaves, rinsed clean	1	teaspoon 30% less fat, real bacon bits
1	medium red onion, sliced into rings and separated	2	strawberries, sliced thinly
1	teaspoon fat-free feta cheese crumbles	1	tablespoon fat-free Italian salad dressing

- Holding all five leaves tightly together, very gently slide the onion ring around all of the leaves (starting at the bottom of the leaves) until it reaches the center of the leaves. Place on a pretty individual serving plate.
- Sprinkle the cheese crumbles, bacon bits, and strawberry slices on top of the leaves. Some cheese, bacon, and strawberry slices will fall onto the plate.
- Cover and keep chilled until ready to serve.
- Drizzle the dressing on top of the salad just before serving.

Yield: 1 serving

Calories: 42 (61% fat); Total Fat: 1 gm; Cholesterol: 3 mg; Carbohydrate: 7 gm; Dietary Fiber: 2 gm; Protein: 3 gm; Sodium: 320 mg
Diabetic Exchanges: 1½ vegetable

Preparation time: 5 minutes or less

Menu Idea: A salad as special as this deserves to be served with a special entrée as well. Lobster tail or crab legs would definitely be extra special.

Red Lettuce Salad

This is another fine example of a fresh garden salad I'm confident you'll enjoy. It is so pretty. You'll be proud serving it instead of the traditional iceberg salad.

1 head red-leaf lettuce, rinsed clean and cut or torn into bite-size pieces	1/4 cup shredded Parmesan cheese (not grated like for spaghetti)
1/2 cup chopped cucumber	10 cherry tomatoes, thinly sliced
5 black olives, cut into thin slices	1/2 cup fat-free red wine vinaigrette salad dressing

- Place the lettuce in a large glass salad bowl.
- Sprinkle the cucumber, black olives, Parmesan cheese, and tomatoes over the lettuce.
- Cover and keep chilled until ready to serve.
- Right before serving, gently toss the salad with the dressing. Serve chilled.
- To make your dinner guests feel a little more special, chill your salad bowls in the freezer so the bowls will be nice and cold for the salad presentation.

Yield: 6 (1½-cup) servings

Calories: 42 (32% fat); Total Fat: 1 gm; Cholesterol: 2 mg; Carbohydrate: 5 gm; Dietary Fiber: 1 gm; Protein: 2 gm; Sodium: 381 mg
Diabetic Exchanges: 1 vegetable

 **Preparation time:** 5 minutes

Menu Idea: This salad is perfect for any home-style entrée such as my Chicken à la King recipe served over low-carb toast on page 121 in *Busy People's Slow Cooker Cookbook* or Herbed Beef Tenderloin on page 151 of the same book.

Bacon, Lettuce & Tomato Slices

If you like bacon, lettuce, and tomato sandwiches, you'll love this.

1 large fresh tomato	1 tablespoon light whipped salad dressing
2 plus 1 tablespoons 30% less fat, real bacon bits	1/2 cup very thinly shredded lettuce (like for tacos)
3 tablespoons fat-free whipped salad dressing	

- Slice the tomato into six slices horizontally. Arrange on a pretty serving plate.
- In a small bowl stir 2 tablespoons bacon bits and the salad dressing together until well mixed.
- With a knife, spread the bacon-salad dressing mixture evenly over the tomato slices.
- Top the tomato slices with the shredded lettuce.
- Sprinkle the lettuce with the remaining 1 tablespoon bacon bits.
- Serve as is, or wrap and keep chilled until ready to eat.

Yield: 3 (2-slice) servings

Calories: 67 (42% fat); Total Fat: 3 gm; Cholesterol: 13 mg; Carbohydrate: 6 gm; Dietary Fiber: 1 gm; Protein: 4 gm; Sodium: 356 mg
Diabetic Exchanges: 1 vegetable, 1/2 very lean meat, 1/2 fat

Preparation time: 10 minutes or less

Menu Idea: Pork Stew in *Busy People's Down-Home Cooking Without the Down-Home Fat* on page 96 is a family favorite that this tomato salad complements nicely.

Cauliflower Salad

This slightly sweet-and-salty flavor combination makes this satisfying salad a special-request dish for family gatherings. I love it because nobody knows it is low-fat, low-calorie, or low-carb. God is so good.

1 cup fat-free mayonnaise	1 small head broccoli florets (about 1½ pounds), finely chopped
½ cup Splenda Granular, measures like sugar	
1 tablespoon apple cider vinegar	½ cup finely chopped red onion
¾ cup 30% less fat, real bacon bits	
2 heads cauliflower (about 3 pounds total), broken into florets, core and stem discarded	

- In a large bowl stir together the mayonnaise, Splenda, vinegar, and bacon until well blended.
- With a large spatula, stir the cauliflower, broccoli, and onion into the dressing.
- Cover and keep chilled until ready to eat.

Note: To save time (but not money), you can purchase cauliflower florets and broccoli florets precut and cleaned in either the produce section or on the salad bar of larger grocery stores.

Yield: 20 (½-cup) servings

Calories: 46 (25% fat); Total Fat: 1 gm; Cholesterol: 7 mg; Carbohydrate: 6 gm; Dietary Fiber: 2 gm; Protein: 3 gm; Sodium: 223 mg
Diabetic Exchanges: 1½ vegetable

Preparation time: 25 minutes or less

Menu Idea: This crunchy salad goes marvelously with the Turkey Cutlets topped with Zesty Cranberry Sauce (with only 7 carbs) on page 216 or the simple Chicken Strips (with only 9 carbs) on page 220, both in *Busy People's Diabetic Cookbook*.

Honey Cucumber Salad

With just a tad of honey, this lightly sweetened, cool, and refreshing salad is a terrific way to use your fresh-from-your-garden cucumbers.

1/2 cup fat-free sour cream
1 tablespoon honey
2 individual packets Splenda
2 large cucumbers, seeded and chopped (about 4 cups)

1/2 cup finely chopped red bell pepper
1/4 cup finely chopped red onion

- In a medium-size serving bowl stir together the sour cream, honey, and Splenda until well mixed.
- Stir in the cucumbers, red pepper, and onions.
- Cover and keep chilled until ready to eat.

Yield: 9 (½-cup) servings

Calories: 35 (0% fat); Total Fat: 0 gm; Cholesterol: 2 mg; Carbohydrate: 7 gm;
Dietary Fiber: 1 gm; Protein: 1 gm; Sodium: 13 mg
Diabetic Exchanges: ½ other carbohydrate

Preparation time: 15 minutes or less

Menu Idea: Two recipes from *Busy People's Diabetic Cookbook*— Chicken with Cool & Creamy Lime Sauce (page 212) with only 9 carbohydrates and Seasoned Buttered Broccoli (page 172) with only 5 carbohydrates—along with this Honey Cucumber Salad make a tasty meal combination.

Southwestern Cucumber Salad

This salad is as versatile as it is fresh and satisfying. It goes well with a vast array of different foods.

1/2 cup chunky salsa	1/4 cup chopped fresh cilantro
1/2 teaspoon ground cumin	2 cucumbers, seeded and chopped
2 individual packets Splenda	(about 5 cups)
1 medium tomato, chopped	
(about 2 cups)	

- In a medium mixing bowl stir together the salsa, cumin, and Splenda until well blended.
- Stir in the tomato, cilantro, and cucumber.
- Cover and keep chilled until ready to eat.

Yield: 14 ($\frac{1}{2}$-cup) servings

Calories: 12 (0% fat); Total Fat: 0 gm; Cholesterol: 0 mg; Carbohydrate: 2 gm;
Dietary Fiber: 1 gm; Protein: 1 gm; Sodium: 41 mg
Diabetic Exchanges: Free

Preparation time: 10 minutes or less

Menu Idea: For dinner have the salad with Breaded Pork Tenderloins on page 184 in *Busy People's Low-fat Cookbook* and Roasted Portabella Mushroom Caps (with only 3 carbs) on page 173 in *Busy People's Diabetic Cookbook*. It also is great on top of tacos, on top of salads, or as a side salad by itself with grilled, lean hamburgers. Last but not least, I like to eat it loaded on fat-free tortilla chips for a light lunch or snack.

Greek-Style Cucumber Salad

Here's the satisfying salad to cure your desire for creamy and crunchy in one dish.

$1/4$ teaspoon garlic salt
$1/2$ tablespoon dried minced onion
$1/4$ teaspoon onion powder
1 cup fat-free sour cream

$1/4$ cup dried parsley or $1/2$ cup finely chopped fresh parsley
$3/4$ cup finely chopped onion
3 cucumbers, seeded and chopped (about 4 cups)

- In a medium-size serving bowl stir together the garlic salt, minced onion, onion powder, sour cream, and parsley until well mixed.
- Stir in the onions and cucumbers.
- Keep chilled until ready to serve.

Yield: 9 ($\frac{1}{2}$-cup) servings

Calories: 54 (0% fat); Total Fat: 0 gm; Cholesterol: 4 mg; Carbohydrate: 10 gm;
Dietary Fiber: 1 gm; Protein: 3 gm; Sodium: 51 mg
Diabetic Exchanges: 1 vegetable, $\frac{1}{2}$ other carbohydrate

 **Preparation time:** 15 minutes or less

 Menu Idea: This salad complements grilled lean meats well. It's also great with Lemon-Herb Chicken Cutlets (with no carbs) on page 213 in *Busy People's Diabetic Cookbook* or as a side salad for a brunch with Puffy Herb Omelet with Cheese (with only 2 carbs) on page 70 in the same cookbook.

Greek-Style Tossed Salad

I used to look forward to eating at Greek restaurants primarily for their renowned Greek salads, which I adore. Unfortunately, most of the restaurants have their salads literally floating in oil. So, I started making my own fast and easy Greek salad versions at home with a fraction of the calories. You'll enjoy this salad.

1	head green leaf lettuce, cut into small, bite-size pieces (about 7 cups)	1/2	medium cucumber, cut into 1/4-inch slices
4	pitted black olives, sliced thinly	2	teaspoons dried parsley or 2 teaspoons chopped fresh parsley
1/3	cup fat-free feta cheese crumbles		
12	cherry tomatoes, quartered	1/2	cup fat-free, red wine vinaigrette salad dressing

- Put the cleaned lettuce in a large salad bowl.
- Top with black olives, feta cheese, quartered tomatoes, and cucumber slices.
- Sprinkle with the parsley.
- Cover and keep chilled until ready to serve.
- Toss with the dressing before serving.

Yield: 5 (1½-cup) servings

Calories: 49 (18% fat); Total Fat: 1 gm; Cholesterol: 0 mg; Carbohydrate: 7 gm;
Dietary Fiber: 1 gm; Protein: 3 gm; Sodium: 535 mg
Diabetic Exchanges: 1½ vegetable,

 **Preparation time:** 10 minutes or less

Menu Idea: This salad goes well with home-style entrées such as Chicken à la King (with 18 carbs) on page 121, or Quick-Fix Chicken (with 18 carbs) on page 138. Both entrées are in the *Busy People's Slow Cooker Cookbook.*

Little Italy Tossed Salad

Here's an attractive yet simple salad appropriate for Italian entrées that are heavily seasoned. This salad will complement Italian and French-based entrées, not overpower them like some salads can.

8	cups (about 1 head) romaine lettuce, cut into bite-size pieces and cleaned	1/4	medium red onion, cut into thin slices and rings separated
10	cherry tomatoes, halved	1/2	cup fat-free Italian salad dressing
10	pitted black olives, sliced	1/3	cup shredded low-fat Parmesan cheese (not grated)
3	radishes, cut into very thin slices		

- Place the romaine lettuce in a large bowl.
- Garnish with the tomatoes, black olives, radishes, and onion. Cover and keep refrigerated until ready to use.
- Just before serving, gently toss the salad with the salad dressing. (Note: Do not put dressing on too far in advance of serving the salad because the salad greens will become soggy and wilted.)
- Sprinkle the Parmesan cheese on top.
- Serve chilled.

Yield: 6 (1½-cup) servings

Calories: 56 (32% fat); Total Fat: 2 gm; Cholesterol: 4 mg; Carbohydrate: 7 gm; Dietary Fiber: 2 gm; Protein: 3 gm; Sodium: 407 mg
Diabetic Exchanges: 1½ vegetable, ½ fat

Preparation time: 15 minutes or less

Menu Idea: This salad goes great with Italian-based meals such as the Italian Mini Meatloaves (page 190) with only 16 carbohydrates in *Busy People's Diabetic Cookbook.*

Italian Vegetable Salad

The Italian-inspired seasonings make boring vegetables robust in this colorful salad.

1¹/₄ cups fat-free Italian salad dressing	4 ounces fresh sliced button mushrooms
6 spears fresh asparagus, cut into 2-inch lengths	¹/₂ cup sliced radishes
1 large cucumber, sliced into ¹/₄-inch slices	1 (8-ounce) package precut fresh broccoli and cauliflower tops
	6 pitted black olives, sliced

- Put the salad dressing in a Ziploc bag with the asparagus, cucumber, mushrooms, radishes, broccoli and cauliflower tops, and olives.
- Seal the bag closed. Gently shake to coat all the vegetables with the dressing. I like to keep this salad in the Ziploc bag versus a bowl because it helps the vegetables throughout the salad incorporate the flavors of the dressing more evenly. Whereas in a bowl, usually the bottom vegetables get more flavor than the vegetables on the top.
- Serve as is, or keep chilled in Ziploc bag until ready to eat.

Yield: 16 (¹/₂-cup) servings

Calories: 25 (16% fat); Total Fat: 1 gm; Cholesterol: 1 mg; Carbohydrate: 4 gm; Dietary Fiber: 1 gm; Protein: 1 gm; Sodium: 289 mg
Diabetic Exchanges: 1 vegetable

Preparation time: 10 minutes or less

Menu Idea: This crunchy salad is good for adding a variety of textures to otherwise tender entrées such as Chicken with Cool & Creamy Lime Sauce (with only 9 carbs) on page 212 of *Busy People's Diabetic Cookbook* or the Sautéed Scallops with Garlic (with only 3 carbs) on page 180 in the same cookbook.

Taco Salad

This is one of my all-time favorite salads. I think you'll agree it's a winner.

1 pound ground eye of round	1 cup (about 4 ounces) shredded fat-free Cheddar cheese
1 (1.25-ounce) package taco seasoning	1 cup finely chopped tomato (about 1 medium tomato)
³/₄ cup water	14 fat-free tortilla chips, crushed
12 cups (about 2 heads) finely shredded iceberg lettuce*	

- In a 12-inch, nonstick skillet, cook and crumble the ground beef.
- Add the taco seasoning mix and the water. Bring to a boil. Reduce the heat to low and simmer for 15 minutes, stirring occasionally. (For an added special flavor, add 1 teaspoon ground cinnamon when you stir in the taco seasoning mix.)
- Put the shredded lettuce in a large bowl and add the cooked taco meat, shredded cheese, tomato, and tortilla chips. Toss together. Serve immediately.

Note: The quickest way to shred this lettuce is with a food processor.

Yield: 4 (3-cup) servings

Calories: 267 (21% fat); Total Fat: 6 gm; Cholesterol: 67 mg; Carbohydrate: 18 gm; Dietary Fiber: 1 gm; Protein: 36 gm; Sodium: 954 mg
Diabetic Exchanges: 1 starch, 1 vegetable, 4 lean meat

Preparation time: 20 minutes or less
Cooking time: 20 minutes or less
Total time: 30 minutes (Preparation can be done while meat is cooking, therefore saving time.)

Menu Idea: This family favorite can be served as a meal or as a side dish. As a side dish it's a nice complement to the Taco Vegetable Soup with 14 carbohydrates in *Busy People's Slow Cooker Cookbook* on page 62.

Yankee-Doodle-Dandy Tossed Salad

The all-American colors of red, white, and blue inspired the name of this unique and tasty salad, perfect to serve on the Fourth of July, especially because blueberries are in season.

1 head romaine lettuce, cleaned and cut into bite-size pieces (about 8 cups)*	1/4 cup low-fat feta cheese, crumbled
1/4 cup 30% less fat, real bacon bits	1/2 cup chopped red bell pepper
1 medium cucumber, peeled, seeded, and chopped (about 1 cup)	1/2 cup fresh blueberries (about 1/4 pint)
	1/3 cup fat-free, red raspberry salad dressing

- In a large glass salad bowl, add the lettuce, bacon, cucumber, feta, red bell pepper, and blueberries.
- Cover and keep chilled until ready to eat.
- Serve with salad dressing on the side.

Note: To save time buy precut and cleaned romaine lettuce.

Yield: 4 (2-cup) servings

Calories: 92 (28% fat); Total Fat: 3 gm; Cholesterol: 13 mg; Carbohydrate: 11 gm; Dietary Fiber: 3 gm; Protein: 7 gm; Sodium: 588 mg
Diabetic Exchanges: 1/2 fruit, 1 vegetable, 1 lean meat

Preparation time: 15 minutes or less

Menu Idea: This is another great little salad to have as a lunch. I had mine with the Banana-Blueberry Milkshake on page 25 of this book. Boy, were those two good together.

Thai Broccoli Salad

Oh, baby! The first bite starts out sweet, but soon becomes spicy hot. Watch out!

2 tablespoons peanut sauce (found in oriental food section with soy sauces)	1 (16-ounce) package broccoli florets (about 4 cups chopped fresh broccoli)
1/3 cup water	1/2 red bell pepper, chopped (about 1/2 cup)
1 tablespoon Splenda Granular, measures like sugar	

- In a medium-size bowl mix together the peanut sauce, water, and Splenda until well blended to make a dressing.
- Add the broccoli and red pepper to the dressing, and gently stir until the broccoli is well coated with dressing.
- Serve as is, or cover and keep chilled until ready to eat.

Yield: 8 (½-cup) servings

Calories: 34 (35% fat); Total Fat: 2 gm; Cholesterol: 0 mg; Carbohydrate: 7 gm; Dietary Fiber: 2 gm; Protein: 2 gm; Sodium: 327 mg
Diabetic Exchanges: 1½ vegetable, ½ fat

Preparation time: 5 minutes or less

Menu Idea: Teriyaki Beef (with only 11 carbs) on page 160 in *Busy People's Slow Cooker Cookbook* is a good choice with this spicy salad.

Oriental Slaw with Mandarin Oranges

The few mandarin oranges in this oriental coleslaw give it just the right amount of added flavor and color to make this a special and unique salad without adding too many carbohydrates.

1 tablespoon lite soy sauce	1 (8-ounce) can sliced water chestnuts, drained and juice discarded
1 tablespoon Splenda Granular, measures like sugar	
2/3 cup sugar-free orange drink	1 (6-ounce) can mandarin oranges in light syrup, syrup drained and discarded
2 tablespoons Teriyaki Baste and Glaze (I use Kikkoman's.)	
1 head Chinese cabbage, very thinly sliced (about 8 cups)	

- In a large salad bowl stir together the soy sauce, Splenda, orange drink, and the Teriyaki Baste and Glaze until well blended.
- Toss together the cabbage, water chestnuts, and mandarin oranges in the dressing.
- Cover and keep chilled until ready to eat.

Yield: 9 ($\frac{1}{2}$-cup) servings

Calories: 34 (0% fat); Total Fat: 0 gm; Cholesterol: 0 mg; Carbohydrate: 7 gm; Dietary Fiber: 1 gm; Protein: 1 gm; Sodium: 201 mg
Diabetic Exchanges: $\frac{1}{2}$ other carbohydrate

Preparation time: 15 minutes or less

Menu Idea: This is good to serve as a unique and flavorful substitute for the traditional high-carbohydrate and high-calorie coleslaw. Try it with Marinated Grilled Chicken (with only 2 carbs) on page 105 in *Busy People's Down-Home Cooking Without the Down-Home Fat.*

Sesame Seed Coleslaw

Unlike other coleslaws, this slaw is not overly sweet or saturated in salad dressing. It is unique in that it gathers its flavors from the wonderful blend of ingredients rather than mostly from the dressing itself.

³/4 cup fat-free red wine vinaigrette salad dressing

3 tablespoons Splenda Granular, measures like sugar

1 (16-ounce) package precut, shredded coleslaw mix (in produce section)

2 green onions, chopped (about ¹/4 cup chopped)

1 tablespoon dried parsley or 2 tablespoons chopped fresh parsley

2 tablespoons sesame seeds, toasted

2 tablespoons slivered almonds, toasted

- In a 1-gallon Ziploc bag put the salad dressing and Splenda together. Seal the bag and shake until the dressing is well blended.
- Add the coleslaw mix, green onions, parsley, sesame seeds, and almonds.
- Close the bag. Shake until all the ingredients are well mixed.
- Keep in the Ziploc bag to help the salad marinate more evenly than if in a bowl.
- Keep refrigerated until ready to eat.

Note: To toast the seeds or almonds broil them on a baking sheet (not at the same time) until toasty golden brown.

Yield: 8 (½-cup) servings

Calories: 57 (35% fat); Total Fat: 2 gm; Cholesterol: 0 mg; Carbohydrate: 7 gm; Dietary Fiber: 2 gm; Protein: 2 gm; Sodium: 327 mg
Diabetic Exchanges: 1½ vegetable, ½ fat

Preparation time: 5 minutes

Menu Idea: This is another great picnic salad that you can serve with Marinated Grilled Chicken Breasts (with only 2 carbs) on page 105 or Steak on a Stick (with only 1 carb) on page 120, both in *Busy People's Down-Home Cooking Without the Down-Home Fat.*

Chilled Green Bean Salad

This sweet-and-sour salad will make you think you are cheating and not eating low-carb because it tastes so good. However, this is a sweet side dish you can indulge in without any guilt. Gee! Isn't that a nice thought? Guilt-free eating. Enjoy!

1 cup fat-free Italian salad dressing	1 (14.5-ounce) can wax beans, drained*
2 tablespoons Spenda Granular	1 (14.5-ounce) can cut green beans, drained*
1/2 cup finely chopped fresh red onion	

- In a medium-size serving bowl mix together the Italian salad dressing and Splenda until well blended.
- Stir in the red onion, wax beans, and green beans.
- Keep chilled until ready to serve.

Note: Time saving idea: When you unload your groceries, put the beans in the refrigerator instead of the cupboard so they will be chilled when you are ready to prepare your salad. This salad tastes best chilled.

Yield: 8 (½-cup) servings

Calories: 43 (0% fat); Total Fat: 0 gm; Cholesterol: 1 mg; Carbohydrate: 8 gm; Dietary Fiber: 1 gm; Protein: 1 gm; Sodium: 773 mg
Diabetic Exchanges: 1½ vegetable

Preparation time: 5 minutes or less

Menu Idea: I served this at a picnic, and it complemented the grilled meats very well. It's also great with Steak on a Stick (with only 1 little carb) on page 120 of *Down-Home Cooking Without the Down-Home Fat.*

Savory Summer Salad

This salad is out-of-this-world-delicious and can be eaten any time of year. It makes a great little lunch by itself.

1	pound skinless, boneless chicken breast, cut into $1/4$ x 2-inch-long strips	2	zucchini, sliced into $1/4$ inch rings (about 3 cups)
1	pound London broil steak, cut into $1/4$ x 2-inch-long strips	1	head romaine lettuce, cut into bite-size pieces
1	plus $3/4$ plus $1/4$ cups fat-free Italian salad dressing (used 3 separate times)	1	plus 1 tablespoons steak seasoning
		1	cup quartered cherry tomatoes

- In a 1 gallon Ziploc bag, combine the chicken strips and steak strips with $3/4$ cup salad dressing. Marinate for 15 minutes.
- In another 1 gallon Ziploc bag combine the zucchini slices with $1/4$ cup salad dressing. Marinate for 13 minutes.
- Preheat a grill to hot.
- In a very large salad bowl toss the romaine lettuce with 1 tablespoon of your favorite steak-seasoning blend. Cover and keep chilled.
- Remove the chicken, steak, and zucchini from the dressing, and cook on the grill. (Discard the dressing that was used as a marinade.)
- Sprinkle the remaining 1 tablespoon steak-seasoning blend lightly over all of the chicken, steak, and zucchini as it grills. Cook both sides of the chicken and steak for 4 to 5 minutes or until the chicken is completely white in the center. Turn the zucchini after 2 to 3 minutes and remove after 4 to 5 minutes. You want the zucchini to be tender, but not overcooked.
- Put the grilled chicken, steak, and zucchini into a 9 x 13-inch pan.

For each salad:

- Put 2 cups seasoned lettuce on a chilled salad plate or bowl.
- Top the lettuce with 2 ounces grilled chicken, 2 ounces grilled steak, $^1/_3$ cup grilled zucchini, and $^1/_8$ cup tomatoes. Drizzle the top of the salad with $1^1/_2$ to 2 tablespoons salad dressing right before serving.

Yield: 8 servings

Calories: 206 (21% fat); Total Fat: 5 gm; Cholesterol: 54 mg; Carbohydrate: 12 gm; Dietary Fiber: 2 gm; Protein: 28 gm; Sodium: 1449 mg
Diabetic Exchanges: 1 vegetable, $^1/_2$ other carbohydrate, 3 lean meat

Preparation time: 20 minutes (including marinating time)
Cooking time: 10 minutes or less
Total time: 30 minutes or less

Menu Idea: This fantastic little salad is just right for lunch with my easy-to-make and super-delicious Raspberry Milkshake on page 26 in this book.

Special Shrimp Salad

All I can say is, "Yum, Yum."

I	tablespoon light soy sauce	$^{1}/_{2}$	cup egg substitute
$^{1}/_{2}$	cup sugar-free lemonade	4	tablespoons chopped red onion
12	ounces cleaned, precooked, shelled large shrimp	2	tablespoons 30% less fat, real bacon bits
12	cups chopped lettuce		

- Put the soy sauce, lemonade, and shrimp in a Ziploc bag. Marinate the shrimp while assembling the salad.
- Place 3 cups lettuce on each of four individual salad plates or bowls.
- Spray a microwave-safe bowl with nonfat cooking spray. Add the egg substitute, cover with wax paper, and cook in the microwave for 1 minute. Stir and cook another 30 seconds. If needed, continue cooking for 10-second intervals until the egg is fully cooked and no longer wet.
- Run cold water over the egg until it is no longer hot. Shake off all the water from the egg and pat dry with a paper towel if needed.
- Mash the egg with a fork to resemble crumbled hard-cooked eggs. Sprinkle 2 tablespoons of the crumbled egg over each salad.
- Sprinkle 1 tablespoon onion and $^{1}/_{2}$ tablespoon bacon bits on each salad.
- Divide the shrimp evenly among the salads.
- Serve each salad with 2 tablespoons of your favorite fat-free dressing if desired.

Yield: 4 (3-cup) servings

Calories: 136 (13% fat); Total Fat: 2 gm; Cholesterol: 171 mg; Carbohydrate: 5 gm;
Dietary Fiber: 0 gm; Protein: 24 gm; Sodium: 509 mg
Diabetic Exchanges: 1 vegetable, 3 very lean meat

Preparation time: 10 minutes

Menu Idea: The Fruity Frothy on page 259 in *Busy People's Low-Fat Cookbook* would be a refreshing beverage that'd be sweet enough to curb your sweet tooth instead of dessert, and it would make for a great lunch.

Strawberry Tossed Salad

This is a very nice looking salad with pretty colors and textures united.

2 plus 1 cups quartered fresh strawberries (about 1 pound total)	1/4 cup chopped onion
1 1/2 heads iceberg lettuce, cut or torn into bite-size pieces (about 8 cups packed)	1/2 cup fat-free red wine vinaigrette salad dressing
1/4 cup 30% less fat, real bacon bits	3 individual packets Splenda
	1 tablespoon walnuts

- In a large salad bowl gently toss 2 cups strawberries, the lettuce, bacon bits, and onion together.
- In a blender put the remaining 1 cup strawberries, the salad dressing, Splenda, and walnuts. Turn the blender on highest speed for 10 seconds. Dressing will be lumpy.
- Toss the salad with the dressing right before serving.

Yield: 5 (1½-cup) servings

Calories: 96 (23% fat); Total Fat: 3 gm; Cholesterol: 8 mg; Carbohydrate: 15 gm; Dietary Fiber: 2 gm; Protein: 5 gm; Sodium: 488 mg
Diabetic Exchanges: ½ fruit, 1½ vegetable, ½ fat

Preparation time: 20 minutes

Menu Idea: The Pork Stew on page 96 in *Busy People's Down-Home Cooking Without the Down-Home Fat* is a good choice with this.

Citrus-Glazed Berry Salad

This sweet, yet slightly tart, berry salad with its unique citrus glaze is delightfully pretty and equally as refreshing to eat.

I plus 5 cups fresh strawberries, cleaned and quartered (about I quart)	1½ cups sugar-free orange drink
	3 tablespoons cornstarch
¾ plus I cup Splenda Granular, measures like sugar	I cup fresh blueberries (about ½ pint)

- In a blender purée 1 cup strawberries, ¾ cup Splenda, the orange drink, and cornstarch.
- Pour into a nonstick saucepan. Cook over medium heat, stirring constantly until thick.
- In a large bowl gently toss the remaining 5 cups strawberries with the blueberries and the remaining 1 cup Splenda.
- Pour the cooked strawberry sauce into a large bowl to cool for about 5 minutes. Then pour it over the sweetened berries. Gently stir, making sure all the berries are thoroughly covered in sauce.
- Cover and chill or serve immediately.

Yield: 14 (½-cup) servings

Calories: 41 (0% fat); Total Fat: 0 gm; Cholesterol: 0 mg; Carbohydrate: 10 gm; Dietary Fiber: 2 gm; Protein: 1 gm; Sodium: 1 mg
Diabetic Exchanges: ½ fruit

Preparation time: 20 minutes or less
Cooking time: 5 minutes or less
Total time: 25 minutes or less

Menu Idea: This will spruce up any boring breakfast, such as scrambled eggs.

Red, White & Blue All-American Fruit Salad

Cool, refreshing, and decorated just right for the Fourth of July or Memorial Day meals. For added fun, insert a lighted sparkler into this dessert right before presenting it to your dining guests. The sparkler will burn for about 30 seconds to 1 minute, adding pizzazz to an otherwise simple salad.

6 cups cubed, seedless watermelon, chilled	1/2 cup fresh blueberries
1/2 teaspoon vanilla extract	1 sparkler firework (optional)
1 cup fat-free dessert whipped topping	

- Put the watermelon in the bottom of a glass trifle bowl.
- In a medium bowl stir the vanilla extract into the whipped topping. Spread over the watermelon.
- Sprinkle with the blueberries.
- Cover and keep refrigerated until ready to eat.
- If desired, put a lighted sparkler in before serving for a dazzling presentation.

Yield: 6 (1-cup) servings

Calories: 74 (0% fat); Total Fat: 0 gm; Cholesterol: 0 mg; Carbohydrate: 17 gm; Dietary Fiber: 1 gm; Protein: 1 gm; Sodium: 8 mg
Diabetic Exchanges: 1 fruit

Preparation time: 7 minutes

Menu Idea: Serve these tasty recipes from *Busy People's Down-Home Cooking Without the Down-Home Fat* : Steak on a Stick on page 120, Red Wine Vinaigrette Cucumber Salad on page 49, and a fresh garden salad with Creamy Blue Cheese Salad Dressing on page 64.

Oriental Spinach Salad

I recommend the homemade Oriental Salad Dressing on the following page.

1/2 cup liquid egg substitute, cooked and crumbled	1 (8-ounce) can sliced water chestnuts, drained
1 (12-ounce) package fresh baby spinach*	4 ounces fresh bean sprouts
	1/4 cup reduced-fat real bacon pieces

- In a microwave-safe bowl sprayed with nonfat cooking spray, cover the egg substitute with wax paper and cook for 1 minute. Stir with a fork. Cover and cook another 30 seconds to 1 minute or until the egg is no longer wet looking.
- Place ice cubes in the bowl with the eggs to cool. Drain the water once the eggs are completely cooled and chilled. With a fork, stir the cooled eggs until crumbly.
- In a large salad bowl toss the spinach with the water chestnuts, egg crumbles, bean sprouts, and bacon pieces.
- Keep chilled until ready to eat.
- Let dining guests top with their favorite salad dressing.

Note: Regular spinach can be used; however, the leaves often are not so tender.

Yield: 4 (1½-cup) servings

Calories: 86 (19% fat); Total Fat: 2 gm; Cholesterol: 10 mg; Carbohydrate: 10 gm; Dietary Fiber: 4 gm; Protein: 10 gm; Sodium: 316 mg
Diabetic Exchanges: 2 vegetable, 1 lean meat

Preparation time: 7 minutes or less

Menu Idea: This flavorful salad often steals the show at meals, so I recommend serving simple and mildly flavored entrées such as grilled or baked fish, chicken, lean beef, or pork.

Oriental Salad Dressing

This salad dressing tastes like a lighter version of a sweet Red French Salad Dressing. Since I created it for the Oriental Salad on the previous page, though, I call it Oriental Salad Dressing. This is one of my very favorite homemade salad dressings.

1 cup water	³/4 cup Splenda Granular, measures like sugar
¹/3 cup ketchup	
¹/4 cup apple cider vinegar	2 tablespoons dried chives or ¹/4 cup chopped fresh chives
1 tablespoon Worcestershire sauce	2 teaspoons lite soy sauce

- Mix the water, ketchup, vinegar, Worcestershire sauce, Splenda, chives, and soy sauce together until well blended.
- Pour into a container and keep chilled.

Yield: 14 (2-tablespoon) servings

Calories: 13 (0% fat); Total Fat: 0 gm; Cholesterol: 0 mg; Carbohydrate: 3 gm; Dietary Fiber: 0 gm; Protein: 0 gm; Sodium: 104 mg
Diabetic Exchanges: Free

Preparation time: 5 minutes or less

Menu Idea: Just because I originally created this dressing for the Oriental Salad on the previous page, don't feel limited to using it only for that salad. I love this dressing on any fresh green tossed salad.

Water Chestnut Salad

The distinctive, crunchy, and nutty texture of this salad tastes good on top of lettuce as well as eaten by itself. It is best eaten the day it is made.

1/4 cup chopped green onion	1 cup fat-free red-wine vinaigrette salad dressing
1 (5-ounce) can sliced water chestnuts, drained and chopped	1/4 teaspoon dried tarragon
1 (8-ounce) package sliced mushrooms (about 2 cups)	1/2 teaspoon dried basil
	1/2 tablespoon dried parsley

- Mix the green onion, water chestnuts, mushrooms, salad dressing, tarragon, basil, and parsley together.
- Serve with a slotted spoon so the salad dressing can drain.

Yield: 4 (1/2-cup) servings

Calories: 64 (0% fat); Total Fat: 0 gm; Cholesterol: 0 mg; Carbohydrate: 13 gm; Dietary Fiber: 3 gm; Protein: 2 gm; Sodium: 828 mg
Diabetic Exchanges: 1 vegetable, 1/2 other carbohydrate

Preparation time: 10 minutes

Menu Idea: Good on top of the Red Lettuce Salad on page 113 in this book, served along with Lemon-Garlic Chicken on page 178 and Spinach and Artichoke Casserole on page 143 in this book.

Sweet Poppy Seed Salad Dressing

This is so easy and inexpensive to make. I don't waste money buying the flavored, bottled dressing anymore; plus it is hard to find a good low-carb poppy seed dressing.

1 cup fat-free sour cream	1/4 cup sugar-free lemonade
1/2 cup Splenda Granular, measures like sugar	1/2 to 1 teaspoon poppy seeds

- In a blender put the sour cream, Splenda, and lemonade. Cover and process on the highest speed for about 1 minute or until well blended and smooth and creamy.
- Stir in the poppy seeds, starting with 1/2 teaspoon and adding more if desired.

Yield: 8 (2-tablespoon) servings

Calories: 42 (0% fat); Total Fat: 0 gm; Cholesterol: 5 mg; Carbohydrate: 8 gm; Dietary Fiber: 0 gm; Protein: 2 gm; Sodium: 25 mg
Diabetic Exchanges: 1/2 other carbohydrate

Preparation time: 5 minutes or less

Menu Idea: Not only is this an excellent sweet dressing to use on fresh green tossed salads, it is equally delicious as a dip for a fresh vegetable tray or as a dip for chicken strips.

Strawberry Feta Dressing

Light, refreshing, and slightly sweetened, this dressing is a very good alternative to the average, boring, low-calorie, low-carb salad dressings.

1	pound fresh strawberries (about ¹/₂ quart), cleaned	6	individual packets Splenda
1	tablespoon apple cider vinegar	2	tablespoons crumbled feta cheese
¹/₂	cup fat-free, low-carb milk		

- On high speed in a blender process the strawberries, vinegar, milk, Splenda, and feta cheese together until smooth and creamy, about 30 to 40 seconds.
- Keep chilled until ready to use.

Yield: 12 (2-tablespoon) servings

Calories: 21 (0% fat); Total Fat: 0 gm; Cholesterol: 2 mg; Carbohydrate: 4 gm; Dietary Fiber: 1 gm; Protein: 1 gm; Sodium: 27 mg
Diabetic Exchanges: Free

Preparation time: 5 minutes or less

Menu Idea: Great on a bed of fresh greens such as Bibb lettuce, romaine lettuce, or iceberg lettuce. Salads topped with this dressing taste especially good with grilled fish or chicken.

Sweet Cheese Dressing

People find it hard to believe this light tasting dressing is low-calorie, low-fat and low-carb. It has just the right amount of sweetness to complement vegetables without overpowering them. Not only do I like it on fresh salad greens but also tossed with fresh broccoli florets or fresh cauliflower florets.

1/2 cup fat-free cottage cheese	1 tablespoon lemon juice
2 tablespoons Splenda Granular, measures like sugar	1/2 teaspoon Mrs. Dash table-blend seasoning
1/3 cup water	

- Put the cottage cheese, Splenda, water, lemon juice, and Mrs. Dash in a blender.
- Put the lid on the blender, and process at highest speed for 2 minutes or until the cottage cheese is no longer lumpy at all.

Yield: 8 (2-tablespoon) servings

Calories: 12 (0% fat); Total Fat: 0 gm; Cholesterol: 1 mg; Carbohydrate: 1 gm; Dietary Fiber: 0 gm; Protein: 2 gm; Sodium: 48 mg
Diabetic Exchanges: Free

Preparation time: 10 minutes or less

Menu Idea: This dressing is perfect for bringing boring fresh veggies alive with flavor. Try it over tomato slices, cherry tomatoes, yellow tomatoes, or broccoli.

Tomato & Bacon Salad Dressing

This sweet-and-sour zesty dressing adds zip to any boring salad greens.

1/2 cup reduced-sodium ketchup	1 cup water
1 tablespoon apple cider vinegar	1/3 cup Splenda Granular, measures like sugar
2 tablespoons dried minced onion	
2 teaspoons paprika	1/3 cup reduced-fat real bacon pieces

- Put the ketchup, vinegar, onion, paprika, water, Splenda, and bacon in a blender.
- Cover and turn the blender on highest speed for 1 minute.
- Serve the dressing on fresh lettuce salads or vegetables.

Yield: 14 (2-tablespoon) servings

Calories: 23 (23% fat); Total Fat: 1 gm; Cholesterol: 4 mg; Carbohydrate: 4 gm; Dietary Fiber: 0 gm; Protein: 1 gm; Sodium: 71 mg
Diabetic Exchanges: Free

Preparation time: 3 minutes or less

Menu Idea: Put on fresh salad greens or assorted vegetables and serve with mild entrées such as grilled fish, steak, pork, or chicken.

Simply Delicious Side Dishes

Spinach & Artichoke Casserole

This kind of reminds me of a thin, no-crust, quiche casserole. I enjoyed the flavor at dinner as a side dish, and the next morning I warmed the leftovers in the microwave for a tasty and satisfying breakfast. It is a very versatile dish.

1 cup fat-free cottage cheese	1 (13.75-ounce) can quartered artichokes hearts, drained
1/4 cup plus 2 tablespoons grated Parmesan cheese	1 (10-ounce) package fresh baby spinach, cleaned
1/2 cup liquid egg substitute	3 green onions, thinly sliced (entire onion except roots)
1/2 plus 1/2 teaspoon lemon-pepper seasoning	

- Preheat the oven to 375 degrees.
- Spray a 9 x 13-inch pan with nonfat cooking spray.
- In a blender process on highest speed (with lid on) the cottage cheese, 1/4 cup Parmesan cheese, egg substitute, and 1/2 teaspoon lemon-pepper seasoning until smooth and creamy.
- Blot the artichokes dry with paper towels.
- In the prepared pan stir together the cheese mixture, artichokes, spinach, and onions.
- Sprinkle the remaining 1/2 teaspoon lemon-pepper seasoning and the remaining 2 tablespoons Parmesan cheese on top of the casserole.
- Bake, uncovered, for 20 minutes or until bubbly hot. Serve hot.

Yield: 7 (1/2-cup) servings

Calories: 76 (17% fat); Total Fat: 1 gm; Cholesterol: 5 mg; Carbohydrate: 6 gm; Dietary Fiber: 2 gm; Protein: 9 gm; Sodium: 390 mg
Diabetic Exchanges: 1 vegetable, 1 very lean meat

Preparation time: 10 minutes or less
Cooking time: 20 minutes
Total time: 30 minutes or less

Menu Idea: As a side dish for lunch this would go great with a cup of soup, such as the Crab & Asparagus Soup (with only 4 carbs) on page 91 of this book.

Zucchini Skillet Dish

Everyone in my family liked this excellent flavor combination, even the children.

1	small onion, chopped (about 1/2 cup)	1	tablespoon ranch salad dressing mix (do not make as directed)
4	cups thinly sliced zucchini (about 4 cups)	2	tablespoons feta cheese crumbles

- Move the oven rack to about 3 inches below the broiler.
- Spray a 12-inch, nonstick skillet with nonfat cooking spray.
- Over medium-high heat cook the onion and zucchini with the lid on for about 5 minutes, stirring occasionally. Preheat the broiler.
- Sprinkle the ranch salad dressing mix over the vegetables, reduce the heat to low, and continue cooking another 3 to 4 minutes.
- Sprinkle the cheese on top of the cooked vegetables, and put the skillet in the oven on the top rack under the broiler for 2 minutes or until the cheese is toasty hot.
- Serve hot.

Yield: 5 (½-cup) servings

Calories: 36 (14% fat); Total Fat: 1 gm; Cholesterol: 1 mg; Carbohydrate: 6 gm; Dietary Fiber: 2 gm; Protein: 2 gm; Sodium: 270 mg
Diabetic Exchanges: 1 vegetable

Preparation time: 5 minutes or less
Cooking time: 10 minutes or less
Total time: 15 minutes or less

Menu Idea: This will be a nice side dish with the Herb Chicken Cutlets (with 0 carbs) on page 214 and a fresh garden tossed salad with the homemade Bacon & Blue Cheese Salad Dressing on page 149, both are found in *Busy People's Diabetic Cookbook*.

Savory Zucchini

My dinner guests ranted and raved about how good they thought this was.

1 medium onion, chopped (or 1 cup frozen chopped onion)	1¹/₂ tablespoons minced garlic
¹/₂ cup fat-free Italian salad dressing	¹/₂ cup finely chopped extra lean ham
3 medium zucchini, cut into ¹/₄-inch slices and then halved	

- In a 12-inch, nonstick skillet cook the onion with the salad dressing over medium-low heat for 4 to 5 minutes with a lid on, stirring occasionally.
- Stir in the zucchini, minced garlic, and ham until well mixed. Cover and cook an additional 4 to 5 minutes, stirring occasionally.
- Serve hot.

Yield: 11 (½-cup) servings

Calories: 32 (15% fat); Total Fat: 1 gm; Cholesterol: 4 mg; Carbohydrate: 5 gm; Dietary Fiber: 1 gm; Protein: 2 gm; Sodium: 239 mg
Diabetic Exchanges: 1 vegetable

Preparation time: 5 minutes or less
Cooking time: 10 minutes or less
Total time: 15 minutes or less

Menu Idea: I like this with Cinnamon-Kissed Chicken (which has only 7 carbs per serving) on page 134 in *Busy People's Slow Cooker Cookbook.*

Zucchini Olé

I thoroughly enjoyed this flavor combination, and if you like spicy foods, I think you will too. Remember, the hotter the salsa, the hotter the dish.

2	medium fresh zucchini, diced (about 5 cups)	1	cup fat-free shredded Cheddar cheese
1	cup salsa		

- Spray a 12-inch nonstick skillet with nonfat cooking spray.
- Cook the zucchini over medium heat with a lid on for 5 to 7 minutes or until tender, stirring occasionally.
- If there is any excess juice, drain the juice and discard. (Depending on your zucchini, you may not need to.)
- Stir in the salsa until well mixed.
- Sprinkle with the cheese.
- Cover and cook for another 1 to 2 minutes or until fully heated.

Yield: 6 (½-cup) servings

Calories: 64 (0% fat); Total Fat: 0 gm; Cholesterol: 3 mg; Carbohydrate: 7 gm; Dietary Fiber: 2 gm; Protein: 8 gm; Sodium: 382 mg
Diabetic Exchanges: 1½ vegetable, 1 very lean meat

Preparation time: 5 minutes
Cooking time: 9 minutes
Total time: 14 minutes or less

Menu Idea: Add zest to your dinner by serving this with Breaded Pork Tenderloins. The Breaded Pork Tenderloins recipe amazingly has only 16 grams of carbohydrates and is found on page 184 in *Busy People's Low-Fat Cookbook.*

Broiled Italian Tomato Slices

The flavor combination is a winning hit.

2	large tomatoes, cut into 6 slices each (12 slices total)	2	ounces fat-free cream cheese
¹/₂	cup fat-free red wine vinaigrette salad dressing	¹/₂	cup chopped fresh green onion tops
2	tablespoons feta cheese	2	teaspoons dried basil
2	tablespoons 30% less fat, real bacon bits		

- Preheat the broiler.
- Line a jelly-roll pan (cookie sheet with ½-inch edge around rim) with foil, and spray the foil with nonfat cooking spray.
- Arrange the tomato slices on the prepared jelly-roll pan.
- Drizzle the slices with the salad dressing.
- In a medium bowl stir together the feta cheese, bacon bits, cream cheese, green onion tops, and dried basil until well mixed.
- Spread about 2 teaspoons of the mixture on top of each tomato slice.
- Broil on the top rack of the oven for 3 to 5 minutes or until the cream cheese is melted.
- Serve hot.

Yield: 6 (2-slice) servings

Calories: 69 (17% fat); Total Fat: 1 gm; Cholesterol: 8 mg; Carbohydrate: 11 gm; Dietary Fiber: 1 gm; Protein: 3 gm; Sodium: 346 mg
Diabetic Exchanges: 1 vegetable, ½ other carbohydrate

Preparation time: 5 minutes or less
Cooking time: 5 minutes or less
Total time: 10 minutes or less

Menu Idea: The Italian Mini Meatloaves (with only 16 carbs) on page 190 in the *Busy People's Diabetic Cookbook* and a tossed Red Lettuce Tossed Salad on page 113 in this book will make a nice, healthy, low-carb, low-fat, low-calorie, yet high in flavor, meal.

Broiled Eggplant Italiano

I am not the biggest fan of eggplant because of its texture. However, I really enjoyed the flavor of this finished product. Those of you who are eggplant fans will enjoy this flavorful recipe very much.

1	eggplant, peeled and sliced vertically into ¹/₂-thick slices	1	(14.5-ounce) can diced tomatoes with basil, garlic, and oregano, drained
¹/₄	plus ¹/₄ cup fat-free zesty Italian salad dressing	1	cup (4 ounces) fat-free shredded mozzarella cheese
1¹/₂	teaspoons Italian seasoning		

- Place the top rack of the oven about 3 inches below the broiler. Preheat the broiler.
- For easy cleanup line a jelly-roll pan with aluminum foil. Spray the foil with nonfat cooking spray.
- Arrange the eggplant slices in a single layer on the prepared pan.
- Drizzle ¼ cup salad dressing over the eggplant slices and then lightly sprinkle them with the Italian seasoning.
- Broil the eggplant for about 3 minutes. Turn the eggplant over and drizzle with ¼ cup salad dressing. Broil an additional 7 minutes or until the eggplant slices are tender.
- Spread the diced tomatoes over all the eggplant, sprinkle the cheese on top, and sprinkle a little more Italian seasoning on the cheese.
- Broil the eggplant again for about 3 minutes or until the cheese is toasty brown. It is very important that you keep your eye on this since the cheese can easily burn.
- Serve hot.

Note: It is best not to use a very big eggplant because they tend to have more seeds and a "spongy texture." Ideally, you want your finished cooked eggplant to be tender.

Yield: 7 (2-slice) servings

Calories: 77 (0% fat); Total Fat: 0 gm; Cholesterol: 3 mg; Carbohydrate: 12 gm;
Dietary Fiber: 1 gm; Protein: 7 gm; Sodium: 746 mg
Diabetic Exchanges: 2 vegetable, ½ very lean meat

Preparation time: 13 minutes or less
Cooking time: 13 minutes
Total time: 26 minutes or less

Menu Idea: Because of the distinct flavors of this dish, I encourage serving a more timid entrée such as the Italian Mini Meatloaves on page 190 in *Busy People's Diabetic Cookbook* or a mild flavored entrée such as the Mushroom & Onion Frittata (with only 12 carbs) on page 91 in *Busy People's Down-Home Cooking Without the Down-Home Fat.*

Dill-Frosted Tomato Slices

This is one of my favorite ways to use fresh-from-the-garden tomatoes.

¹/₄ cup fat-free sour cream	1 large fresh tomato, sliced into 6 slices
2 tablespoons fat-free whipped salad dressing	¹/₂ teaspoon dried dill or 1 teaspoon fresh dill
1 teaspoon ranch salad dressing mix (do not make as directed)	
1 teaspoon dried chives or 2 teaspoons fresh chopped chives	

- In a medium bowl with a spatula, mix together the sour cream, salad dressing, ranch salad dressing mix, and chives until smooth, creamy, and well blended.
- Arrange the tomato slices on a serving plate.
- With a butter knife, spread the seasoned cream mixture over the top of the sliced tomatoes.
- Sprinkle the tops with dill.
- Serve chilled.

Yield: 3 (2-slice) servings

Calories: 48 (0% fat); Total Fat: 0 gm; Cholesterol: 3 mg; Carbohydrate: 9 gm; Dietary Fiber: 1 gm; Protein: 2 gm; Sodium: 259 mg
Diabetic Exchanges: ¹/₂ starch

Preparation time: 10 minutes or less

Menu Idea: These are especially yummy with produce fresh from the garden; and this makes having the Ham & Cabbage Dinner (with only 13 grams of carbs) found on page 198 in *Busy People's Low-Fat Cookbook* wonderful, because cabbage and tomatoes are in season at the same time. Yippee!

Ranch Green Beans

The red color of the bell peppers sprinkled throughout, along with the savory flavors of the sausage, fuse a dish full of flavor and appeal.

1/4 cup finely chopped red bell pepper	1 cup sausage-flavored Ground Meatless*
2 (14-ounce) cans green beans, drained	2 tablespoons fat-free liquid creamer

- In a nonstick saucepan cook the bell pepper, green beans, sausage, and creamer together until fully heated over medium heat, stirring occasionally.
- Serve hot.

Note: Ground Meatless is a vegetarian meat substitute made by Morningstar Farms. It's found in the freezer section of your grocery store. If desired, you can use cooked and crumbled turkey Italian sausage instead, but the nutritional information will be different.

Yield: 6 (½-cup) servings

Calories: 49 (14% fat); Total Fat: 1 gm; Cholesterol: 0 mg; Carbohydrate: 7 gm; Dietary Fiber: 2 gm; Protein: 4 gm; Sodium: 538 mg
Diabetic Exchanges: 1½ vegetable

Preparation time: 4 minutes
Cooking time: 6 minutes or less
Total time: 10 minutes or less

Menu Idea: These beans have a robust flavor because of the sausage, so I recommend mild entrées from this cookbook such as the Sweet Onion Marinated Chicken (page 184) or the Slow-Roasted Cornish Hens (page 213).

Savory Seasoned Green Beans

I can't think of a quicker recipe to spruce up boring green beans into a flavorful dish more than this one.

2 ounces reduced-fat cream cheese, cut into ¹/₂-inch cubes	1 (28-ounce) can green beans, not drained
2 teaspoons ranch mix (do not make as directed)	Pinch of celery salt

- Mix the cream cheese, ranch mix, green beans, and celery salt in a microwave-safe dish.
- Cover and microwave for 2 minutes.
- Stir and serve hot.

Yield: 7 (½-cup) servings

Calories: 42 (38% fat); Total Fat: 2 gm; Cholesterol: 6 mg; Carbohydrate: 5 gm;
Dietary Fiber: 1 gm; Protein: 2 gm; Sodium: 555 mg
Diabetic Exchanges: 1 vegetable, ½ fat

Preparation time: 5 minutes

Menu Idea: Serve this with Barbequed Chicken with Corn on the Cob (with only 18 carbs) on page 119 in *Busy People's Slow Cooker Cookbook.*

Greek-Style Green Beans

This is another one of those terrific side dishes I created and enjoyed so much that I made a vegetarian dinner out of it for myself. The flavor combination is spectacular.

1/2 cup chopped red onion	1/4 cup feta cheese, broken into small crumbles
1/2 teaspoon dried oregano	
1/4 cup fat-free red wine vinaigrette salad dressing	5 black olives, pitted and cut into thin slices
2 (14.5-ounce) cans green beans, drained	

- Adjust the top rack of the oven about 3 inches from the top and preheat the broiler.
- In a 9 x 9-inch, glass dish cook the onions and oregano in the salad dressing covered with wax paper in the microwave for about 1 minute or until the onions are tender.
- Stir in the green beans and coat well with the dressing. Cover with wax paper. Cook in the microwave an additional 2 minutes.
- Sprinkle the feta cheese on top and add the sliced olives.
- Broil for about 3 minutes or until the top of the cheese is lightly browned, watching closely so it does not burn.
- Serve hot.

Yield: 6 (1/2-cup) servings

Calories: 63 (25% fat); Total Fat: 2 gm; Cholesterol: 6 mg; Carbohydrate: 10 gm; Dietary Fiber: 1 gm; Protein: 2 gm; Sodium: 659 mg
Diabetic Exchanges: 2 vegetable, 1/2 fat

Preparation time: 5 minutes
Cooking time: 6 minutes
Total time: 11 minutes or less

Menu Idea: Entrées such as the Crab Skillet Dinner (page 169) or the Sweet Onion Marinated Chicken (page 184) or the Sensational Bay Scallops (page 165) in this book would all taste delicious with these beans.

Zucchini & Onions

This tasted so fantastic I had numerous servings for a vegetarian dinner that was every bit as good as a great steak, and I love a great steak.

1	tablespoon light butter	$1/2$	teaspoon garlic salt
1	large onion, cut into $1/8$-inch slices		Dash of freshly ground black pepper (optional)
3	small zucchini, cut into $1/4$-inch slices (about 5 cups)		

- Spray a 12-inch, nonstick skillet with nonfat cooking spray.
- Melt the butter over medium-high heat.
- Once the butter has melted, add the onions to the skillet. Cover and cook the onions for 5 to 7 minutes, or until the onions begin to caramelize and turn brown, stirring occasionally.
- Add the zucchini and garlic salt. Cover and cook an additional 5 to 7 minutes, or until the zucchini is tender, stirring occasionally.
- Sprinkle lightly with a dash of the black pepper if desired.
- Serve hot.

Yield: 8 (½-cup) servings

Calories: 23 (28% fat); Total Fat: 1 gm; Cholesterol: 2 mg; Carbohydrate: 4 gm; Dietary Fiber: 1 gm; Protein: 1 gm; Sodium: 74 mg
Diabetic Exchanges: 1 vegetable

Preparation time: 6 minutes or less
Cooking time: 14 minutes
Total time: 20 minutes or less

Menu Idea: Slow Roasted, Marinated London Broil on page 212 in this book with the Greek-Style Tossed Salad on page 119, also in this book makes a low-carb meal you'll think is high-carb by how delicious it tastes.

Nacho Cucumber Slices

As we say in Spanish, this is a bueno *(good) side dish for southwestern or Mexican-theme meals.*

1 **cup thick and chunky salsa**	1/2 **cup finely shredded fat-free Cheddar cheese**
1 **medium cucumber, cut into** 1/4**-inch slices**	1/2 **cup fat-free sour cream**

- Place the salsa in a strainer to drain the excess juice. Set aside to let the salsa drain while preparing the cucumbers. Discard the excess juice.
- Arrange the sliced cucumbers in a 9 x 13-inch glass casserole dish or large platter (with a 1/2-inch edge so the juices won't drain off).
- Top each cucumber slice with 1 teaspoon salsa.
- Sprinkle the salsa-topped cucumber slices lightly with the cheese and add about 1 teaspoon sour cream on top of each slice.
- Cover and keep chilled until ready to eat.

Yield: 7 (3-slice) servings

Calories: 49 (0% fat); Total Fat: 0 gm; Cholesterol: 4 mg; Carbohydrate: 6 gm; Dietary Fiber: 0 gm; Protein: 4 gm; Sodium: 251 mg
Diabetic Exchanges: 1 vegetable, 1/2 very lean meat

Preparation time: 10 minutes or less

Menu Idea: This is an *excellente* side dish for the Taco Lettuce Wraps (page 196 in this book) served with the Fruit Punch (page 202) with only 4 carbohydrates from *Busy People's Down-Home Cooking Without the Down-Home Fat.*

Garlic Cucumbers

These cool, refreshing, and crunchy cucumbers are best eaten the day they are prepared. After a few days the cucumbers get watery and lose their firm and crunchy texture.

1	medium cucumber, cut into 21 slices	1	tablespoon plus 1 teaspoon dried chives
4	ounces fat-free cream cheese, softened	1	teaspoon ranch salad dressing mix (do not make as directed)
1/2	cup fat-free sour cream	1/4	teaspoon garlic salt with parsley
1 1/2	tablespoons minced garlic (from a jar is fine)		

- Arrange the sliced cucumbers in a 9 x 13-inch glass casserole dish or large platter.
- In a medium-size bowl with an electric mixer beat together the cream cheese, sour cream, minced garlic, 1 tablespoon chives, and the salad dressing mix until well blended and smooth.
- Sprinkle the cucumber slices lightly with the garlic salt.
- Put the cream cheese mix into a frosting bag (or into a small plastic bag with the tip of a corner cut off).
- Squeeze a dab of the mix onto the top of each cucumber slice in the center.
- Sprinkle all of the tops lightly with the remaining 1 teaspoon chives.
- Cover and keep chilled until ready to eat.

Yield: 7 (3-slice) servings

Calories: 48 (0% fat); Total Fat: 0 gm; Cholesterol: 6 mg; Carbohydrate: 7 gm; Dietary Fiber: 0 gm; Protein: 4 gm; Sodium: 212 mg
Diabetic Exchanges: 1/2 other carbohydrate, 1/2 very lean meat

Preparation time: 10 minutes or less

Menu Idea: This crunchy side dish is great on hot days with grilled entrées such as Grilled & Lightly Barbequed Shrimp Kebabs on page 168 in this book.

Confetti-Topped Asparagus

Tender asparagus topped with finely diced red bell pepper, mushrooms, and ham make this a vibrant, colorful side dish. It is every bit as tasty as it is pretty.

1 **pound fresh small asparagus spears with ends cut off (about 30 asparagus spears)***	1/3 **cup finely diced fresh mushrooms**
1 **cup sugar-free lemonade**	1/3 **cup finely diced extra lean ham**
1/3 **cup finely diced fresh red bell pepper**	1/8 **teaspoon garlic salt**

- In a large nonstick skillet cook the asparagus in lemonade over high heat with the lid on for 5 minutes or until asparagus is tender.
- Remove the asparagus and put them in a covered dish.
- Add the red bell pepper, mushrooms, ham, and garlic salt to the lemonade in the skillet. Cook on high and allow the mixture to boil with the lid off for another 5 minutes, stirring peppers, mushrooms, and ham occasionally.
- Pour the contents of the skillet over the asparagus.
- Serve immediately with a slotted spoon so the juice can drain.

Note: Thin asparagus spears are more tender than larger asparagus.

Yield: 4 servings (about 7 spears with ¼ cup cooked bell pepper, mushrooms, and ham)

Calories: 53 (12% fat); Total Fat: 1 gm; Cholesterol: 6 mg; Carbohydrate: 6 gm; Dietary Fiber: 3 gm; Protein: 5 gm; Sodium: 171 mg
Diabetic Exchanges: 1 vegetable, ½ very lean meat

Preparation time: 5 minutes or less
Cooking time: 10 minutes
Total time: 15 minutes or less

Menu Idea: I like this with heavier based entrées such as grilled steak. The Pork Tenderloin (with only 10 carbs) on page 172 in *Busy People's Slow Cooker Cookbook* is another good choice as well.

Cauliflower with Herbs

I like this as it is. However, Amy, a friend of mine, suggested mashing the cauliflower so it will resemble mashed potatoes.

1 head cauliflower, cut or broken into bite-size pieces (or 2 pounds frozen cauliflower)	1 tablespoon minced garlic
	1/4 teaspoon light salt
1 (14-ounce) can fat-free, reduced-sodium chicken broth*	1 tablespoon dried parsley or 2 tablespoons chopped fresh parsley
1 tablespoon horseradish	
1 tablespoon reduced-fat butter, softened	

- Cook the cauliflower and chicken broth, covered, over medium heat for 10 to 12 minutes or until the cauliflower is tender.
- While the cauliflower is cooking, stir the horseradish, butter, garlic, salt, and parsley together in a serving bowl until well blended.
- When the cauliflower is done, drain and discard the chicken broth.
- Gently mix the cauliflower in with the herb seasoning with a spatula.
- Serve hot.

Note: You can substitute 2 chicken bullion cubes dissolved in 2 cups water for the chicken broth if desired.

Yield: 11 (½-cup) servings

Calories: 24 (30% fat); Total Fat: 1 gm; Cholesterol: 2 mg; Carbohydrate: 3 gm; Dietary Fiber: 1 gm; Protein: 2 gm; Sodium: 202 mg
Diabetic Exchanges: 1 vegetable

Preparation time: 10 minutes or less (if using fresh cauliflower)
Cooking time: 12 minutes or less
Total time: 22 minutes or less

Menu Idea: The Beef & Mushroom Gravy over Potatoes (with only 21 carbs per entrée) on page 141 in *Busy People's Slow Cooker Cookbook* is an excellent choice to serve with this recipe. If you want a complete meal with lower carbohydrates, simply omit the potatoes.

Try-to-Fool-'Em Angel Hair Pasta

This is a good substitute base for pasta such as spaghetti or angel hair. Serve your favorite low-carb spaghetti sauce over this.

1 head of cabbage	1 (14-ounce) can fat-free, reduced-sodium chicken broth

- Cut the core out of the cabbage and discard. Remove any blemished cabbage leaves and discard them as well.
- With a food processor, cut the cabbage up into very thin, fine shreds.
- Separate the shredded cabbage so it is not at all clumped together.
- Pour the chicken broth into the bottom of a 5-quart or larger soup pot.
- Place the shredded cabbage in a pot with the chicken broth.
- Cover and cook on medium-high for about 6 to 10 minutes or until tender, but not mushy or overcooked.
- Drain and discard the broth.
- Serve hot.

Note: The number of servings depends on the size of the cabbage. Regardless of how many servings you get from your head of cabbage, the nutritional information per serving of steamed cabbage will remain the same.

Yield: 8 (1-cup) servings

Calories: 43 (0% fat); Total Fat: 0 gm; Cholesterol: 0 mg; Carbohydrate: 8 gm; Dietary Fiber: 3 gm; Protein: 2 gm; Sodium: 110 mg
Diabetic Exchanges: 1½ vegetable

Preparation time: 5 minutes
Cooking time: 8 minutes
Total time: 13 minutes

Menu Idea: Top with low-carb spaghetti sauce, and have a serving of lean protein such as low-fat turkey Italian sausage. Add a tossed salad for a complete meal.

Turnip Greens with Ham

My girlfriend, Kathy Johnson, who has six children, helped retest this recipe for me. Her note read: "My kids loved this. *Wow!*"

2 (14-ounce) cans turnip greens, drained	2 tablespoons imitation butter-flavored sprinkles (in the spice section of store)
1 (8-ounce) package extra-lean ham, finely chopped	1 individual packet Splenda
1/4 teaspoon ground black pepper	

- In a 12-inch, nonstick skillet with the lid on, cook the turnip greens and ham over medium heat for 5 to 10 minutes or until fully heated, stirring occasionally.
- Stir in the pepper, butter-flavored sprinkles, and Splenda.
- Serve hot.

Yield: 6 (½-cup) servings

Calories: 79 (26% fat); Total Fat: 2 gm; Cholesterol: 20 mg; Carbohydrate: 6 gm; Dietary Fiber: 2 gm; Protein: 10 gm; Sodium: 941 mg
Diabetic Exchanges: 1 vegetable, 1 lean meat

Preparation time: 5 minutes
Cooking time: 8 minutes
Total time: 13 minutes

Menu Idea: The Chicken-Fried Steak (with only 14 carbs) on page 204, the Hens & Eggs Tossed Salad (with only 2 carbs) on page 145, and the Sugar-Free Lemon Meringue Cookies (with only 1 tiny carb) on page 243 are all in *Busy People's Diabetic Cookbook* and will accompany this vegetable dish wonderfully.

On the Go Entrées

*Indicates a slow cooker recipe

Basil & Garlic Shrimp & Scallops

The mild flavors of these ingredients complement each other.

I tablespoon light butter	I (20-ounce) bag frozen bay scallops
I teaspoon Mrs. Dash Tomato-Basil Seasoning blend	I (16-ounce) bag cleaned and fully-cooked frozen, salad shrimp, thawed
I tablespoon minced garlic (from a jar)	

- In a 12-inch, nonstick skillet, melt the butter with the tomato-basil seasoning and garlic over medium heat.
- Add the scallops. Cook for about 3 minutes. Turn the scallops over. Continue cooking for another 2 to 3 minutes, or until the scallops are white throughout.
- Add the shrimp.
- Cover, reduce the heat to low, and cook 1 minute, or until the shrimp are fully heated.
- Remove from the heat and serve immediately.

Yield: 4 (⅔-cup) servings

Calories: 253 (14% fat); Total Fat: 4 gm; Cholesterol: 273 mg; Carbohydrate: 4 gm; Dietary Fiber: 0 gm; Protein: 48 gm; Sodium: 500 mg
Diabetic Exchanges: 6 very lean meat

Preparation time: 5 minutes
Cooking time: 10 minutes
Total time: 15 minutes

Menu Idea: I liked the crunchiness that the Nacho Cucumber Slices (page 155) added to this meal when I ate them for dinner along with the Red Lettuce Salad (page 113), both found in this book.

Scallops in Tomato Cream Sauce

A smooth tomato cream sauce with the sweet and distinct flavor only small bay scallops provide.

2 **(12-ounce) bags frozen bay scallops**	$1/8$ **teaspoon Splenda Granular, measures like sugar**
$1/4$ **cup ketchup**	$1/2$ **teaspoon dried parsley flakes**
2 **tablespoons mustard**	

- Spray a 12-inch, nonstick skillet with nonfat cooking spray.
- Cook the scallops in the prepared skillet over medium-high heat, stirring frequently. As the scallops cook they will release a milky liquid.
- Scallops are fully cooked when they are whitish in color and tender. This will take only a few minutes, because they cook quickly. Remove the scallops with a slotted spoon, and place them in a covered dish to keep warm.
- Add the ketchup, mustard, Splenda, and parsley to the liquid in the skillet. With a whisk, briskly stir the ingredients together until well blended.
- Return the scallops to the skillet with the sauce. Cook only a minute or less, just enough to heat and coat the scallops in the sauce.
- Serve hot.

Yield: 4 ($1/2$-cup) servings

Calories: 169 (9% fat); Total Fat: 2 gm; Cholesterol: 56 mg; Carbohydrate: 8 gm; Dietary Fiber: 0 gm; Protein: 29 gm; Sodium: 525 mg
Diabetic Exchanges: $1/2$ other carbohydrate, 5 very lean meat

Preparation time: 5 minutes or less
Cooking time: 5 minutes
Total time: 10 minutes or less

Menu Idea: The Cucumber Salad with Bacon & Blue Cheese (with 7 carbs) on page 148 in *Busy People's Diabetic Cookbook* along with the Wilted Fresh Spinach with Herbs (with only 3 carbs) on page 171, also in *Busy People's Diabetic Cookbook,* makes this a meal worth remembering and requested again and again.

Sensational Bay Scallops

Sometimes the simplest recipes are the tastiest. This wonderfully delicious scallop recipe with its mild, yet distinct, taste is no exception. The flavor is simply sensational. I've tried scallops prepared in many exquisite and time-consuming ways, but I still think this is the best.

1	tablespoon light butter	1	teaspoon dried dill weed
1	(12-ounce) bag frozen bay scallops*, thawed and juices drained		

- In a medium, nonstick skillet melt the butter over medium-high heat.
- As soon as you have about a 2-inch circle of melted butter in the bottom of your skillet, add the scallops and dill.
- Constantly stir the scallops for 2 to 3 minutes, or until they are opaque in color and lightly coated with the dill and the butter is a milky color with flecks of dill throughout.
- Serve hot.

*Note: I recommend and prefer bay scallops because they are small, super tender, and melt-in-your-mouth delicious. You don't have to worry about bay scallops being gritty like larger scallops sometimes are.

Yield: 3 (4-ounce) servings

Calories: 117 (23% fat); Total Fat: 3 gm; Cholesterol: 44 mg; Carbohydrate: 3 gm; Dietary Fiber: 0 gm; Protein: 19 gm; Sodium: 207 mg
Diabetic Exchanges: 3 very lean meat

Preparation time: 2 minutes
Cooking time: 5 minutes or less
Total time: 7 minutes

Menu Idea: For a special dinner I recommend serving Deviled Eggs (with only 1 carb) on page 47 and the California Garlic Blend on page 120, both of which are in *Busy People's Low-Fat Cookbook*.

Shrimp & Scallops in Tomato Cream Sauce

This delectable sauce reminds me of a smooth homemade tomato soup, but thicker, richer, and creamier.

12 ounces frozen bay scallops	12 ounces frozen shrimp, cleaned, deveined, and tails removed
1 tablespoon cornstarch	1 teaspoon dried parsley
1 cup fat-free, low-carb milk	1/2 teaspoon Old Bay seasoning
1/4 cup ketchup	

- Cook the scallops in a skillet coated with nonstick cooking spray over medium heat, stirring frequently for 3 to 5 minutes or until opaque. With a slotted spoon, remove the scallops from the skillet and place them on a covered plate to keep warm.
- In a cup stir the cornstarch in the milk until completely dissolved.
- Add the milk mixture and ketchup to the scallop juices in the skillet. Stir constantly with a whisk over medium heat until thickened, about 3 minutes.
- Add the shrimp and cook, covered, for 2 to 3 minutes. Add the scallops and cook, covered, until fully heated.
- Reduce the heat, remove the lid, and cook at a low simmer until the cream sauce is at desired consistency.
- Stir in Old Bay seasoning and parsley and serve hot.

Yield: 5 (2/3-cup) servings

Calories: 143 (8% fat); Total Fat: 1 gm; Cholesterol: 124 mg; Carbohydrate: 7 gm; Dietary Fiber: 0 gm; Protein: 25 gm; Sodium: 465 mg
Diabetic Exchanges: 1/2 other carbohydrate, 3 1/2 very lean meat

Preparation time: 5 minutes
Cooking time: 6 minutes
Total time: 11 minutes

Menu Idea: Because this is somewhat expensive to prepare I suggest saving it for special occasions served with the Fancy-Shmancy Salad (page 112) and Savory Zucchini (page 145) both from this book.

Chilled Citrus Shrimp

These marinated shrimp have a very light sweet and sour flavor that complements and enhances the flavor of the shrimp. This light marinade is not overpowering like a lot of heavy sweet and sour sauces can be.

1 **tablespoon light soy sauce**	2 **tablespoons Teriyaki Baste and Glaze (I use Kikkoman's found in the barbeque aisle.)**
1 **tablespoon Splenda Granular, measures like sugar**	
²/₃ **cup sugar-free orange drink**	1 **(12-ounce) bag frozen shrimp, cleaned, shelled, and deveined**

- Put the soy sauce, Splenda, orange drink, and Teriyaki Baste and Glaze in a 1-gallon Ziploc bag. Seal the bag shut and shake until well blended.
- Add the shrimp and marinate for at least 15 minutes in the refrigerator.
- Serve the shrimp chilled with the marinade on the side as a dip.

Yield: 3 (4-ounce) servings

Calories: 135 (9% fat); Total Fat: 1 gm; Cholesterol: 221 mg; Carbohydrate: 5 gm; Dietary Fiber: 0 gm; Protein: 24 gm; Sodium: 726 mg
Diabetic Exchanges: ¹/₂ other carbohydrate, 3 very lean meat

Preparation time: (including marinating time): 20 minutes or less

Menu Idea: These shrimp are equally delicious as an appetizer before seafood-based entrées. As an entrée, they go well with a large, tossed, fresh green garden salad topped with my wonderful Creamy Blue Cheese Salad Dressing (with only 4 little carbs) on page 64 in *Busy People's Down-Home Cooking Without the Down-Home Fat.*

Grilled & Lightly Barbequed Shrimp Kebabs

Diluting the high-in-carbohydrate-barbeque sauce with the carbohydrate-free lemonade is a clever way to stretch your carbohydrates without sacrificing flavor.

½ cup barbeque sauce ½ cup sugar-free lemonade	1 pound large frozen and cooked shrimp, cleaned and shells removed

- Preheat a grill to medium hot.
- In a 1-gallon Ziploc bag put the barbeque sauce and lemonade together.
- With 6 shrimp per skewer put the skewered shrimp in the bag and marinate at least 15 minutes.
- Grill the marinated shrimp skewers for about 2 minutes per side. Drizzle sauce over the kebabs while grilling.
- Put the remaining sauce in the microwave for 1 minute, or until it comes to a low boil. Serve the remaining sauce on the side as a dip if desired.

Yield: 4 (4-ounce) kebabs

(with sauce) Calories: 174 (7% fat); Total Fat: 1 gm; Cholesterol: 221 mg; Carbohydrate: 13 gm; Dietary Fiber: 0 gm; Protein: 24 gm; Sodium: 465 mg
Diabetic Exchanges: 1 other carbohydrate, 4 very lean meat
(without sauce) Calories: 112 (10% fat); Total Fat: 1 gm; Cholesterol: 221 mg; Carbohydrate: 0 gm; Dietary Fiber: 0 gm; Protein: 24 gm; Sodium: 254 mg
Diabetic Exchanges: 4 very lean meat

Preparation time: 25 minutes or less
Cooking time: 5 minutes
Total time: 30 minutes or less

Menu Idea: Since they are already fully cooked, these marinated shrimp also taste great served on a fresh, tossed salad. Grilled, they taste great with Tropical Cabbage on page 80 in *Busy People's Slow Cooker Cookbook.*

Crab Skillet Dinner

This was a huge hit at our home. My daughters even liked the leftovers served cold on crackers.

¹/₂ cup chopped onion	1 pound crabmeat, fully cooked*, finely chopped, and shredded
2 celery stalks, finely chopped (about ²/₃ cup)	¹/₂ cup light whipped salad dressing
1 tablespoon minced garlic	
1 tablespoon Worcestershire sauce	¹/₄ cup shredded Parmesan cheese

- In a 12-inch nonstick skillet that has been sprayed with nonfat cooking spray over medium-high heat, cook the onion, celery, garlic, and Worcestershire sauce for about 5 minutes or until the onion is tender.
- Stir in the crabmeat and whipped salad dressing until well mixed.
- Sprinkle with the shredded Parmesan cheese.
- Cover, reduce the heat to medium-low, and cook for 2 to 3 minutes or until the cheese is melted on top.
- Serve hot.

Note: Do not use canned crabmeat. Imitation crab is fine, but it is higher in carbohydrates.

Yield: 4 (1-cup) servings

(with real crab) Calories: 237 (34% fat); Total Fat: 9 gm; Cholesterol: 98 mg; Carbohydrate: 10 gm; Dietary Fiber: 0 gm; Protein: 28 gm; Sodium: 835 mg Diabetic Exchanges: ¹/₂ other carbohydrate, 3 lean meat
(with imitation crab) Calories: 226 (36% fat); Total Fat: 9 gm; Cholesterol: 53 mg; Carbohydrate: 19 gm; Dietary Fiber: 0 gm; Protein: 17 gm; Sodium: 1206 mg Diabetic Exchanges: 1¹/₂ other carbohydrate, 3 lean meat

Preparation time: 5 minutes
Cooking time: 10 minutes
Total time: 15 minutes

Menu Idea: Because real crabmeat is so expensive, I usually make a special dinner out of this by starting out with the Fancy-Shmancy Salad on page 112 in this book. For an appetizer I serve the Spinach & Artichoke Dip (with only 6 carbs) on page 105, in *Busy People's Diabetic Cookbook*.

Cajun Crab Skillet Dinner

Every once in a while I create a dish that tastes better than I anticipated it would. This is such a dish. I know you'll enjoy it every bit as much as my family, friends, and I do.

2 celery stalks, finely chopped (about 1 cup)	1/2 cup fat-free mayonnaise
1/4 cup diced chilies (about half a 4-ounce can)	1/2 teaspoon mustard
1 pound crabmeat, fully cooked, chopped, and shredded*	1/2 teaspoon Cajun seasoning
	1/4 cup finely shredded hot pepper cheese

- In a 12-inch, nonstick skillet sprayed with nonfat cooking spray, cook the celery with the chilies, covered, over medium-high heat for 4 to 5 minutes or until the celery is tender.
- Stir in the crabmeat, mayonnaise, mustard, and Cajun seasoning until well mixed.
- Sprinkle the top with the cheese. Reduce the heat to medium-low, cover, and cook for 4 to 6 minutes or until the cheese is melted.
- Serve hot.

Note: To cut cost, imitation crabmeat can be substituted; however, notice the carbohydrate and nutritional difference below.

Yield: 3 (1-cup) servings

(with real crab) Calories: 242 (24% fat); Total Fat: 6 gm; Cholesterol: 129 mg; Carbohydrate: 9 gm; Dietary Fiber: 2 gm; Protein: 36 gm; Sodium: 1121 mg
Diabetic Exchanges: 1/2 other carbohydrate, 5 lean meat
(with imitation crab) Calories: 229 (24% fat); Total Fat: 6 gm; Cholesterol: 45 mg; Carbohydrate: 23 gm; Dietary Fiber: 2 gm; Protein: 21 gm; Sodium: 1821 mg
Diabetic Exchanges: 1 1/2 other carbohydrate, 3 very lean meat

Preparation time: 10 minutes
Cooking time: 13 to 15 minutes
Total time: 25 minutes or less

Menu Idea: The Tomato Zing Salad (with only 6 carbs) on page 52 in *Busy People's Down-Home Cooking Without the Down-Home Fat* along with a fresh green lettuce salad will make this entrée a great meal.

Cream Cheese & Crab Frittata

This is one of my all-time favorite meals. Excellent! It tastes a lot like a quiche without a crust.

1/2 teaspoon imitation butter flavoring (found near vanilla extract)	1 tablespoon fat-free whipped salad dressing
1 cup liquid egg substitute (or 8 egg whites beaten)	1 pound imitation crabmeat, cut into bite-size pieces and shredded
1/2 teaspoon garlic salt	4 ounces reduced-fat cream cheese, cut into 1/4-inch pieces

- Preheat the oven to 400 degrees.
- Spray a 12-inch, nonstick skillet with nonfat cooking spray.
- With the heat off stir the butter flavoring, egg, garlic salt, and whipped salad dressing together in a skillet until well blended.
- Turn the heat to medium and gently stir in the crab and cream cheese chunks.
- Reduce the heat to medium low, cover, and cook for 10 minutes.
- Remove the lid. Place the skillet on the top rack of the oven. Bake for 10 to 13 minutes or until it is no longer wet on top.
- Cut into six pie-shape pieces.
- Serve hot.

Yield: 6 servings

Calories: 147 (31% fat); Total Fat: 5 gm; Cholesterol: 28 mg; Carbohydrate: 9 gm; Dietary Fiber: 0 gm; Protein: 15 gm; Sodium: 900 mg
Diabetic Exchanges: 1/2 other carbohydrate, 2 lean meat

Preparation time: 5 minutes
Cooking time: 23 minutes
Total time: 28 minutes or less

Menu Idea: In *Busy People's Slow Cooker Cookbook* on page 102 try the Bacon Green Beans (with only 10 carbs per serving) that'd go great with this, as well as the Mint Tea (with only 1 carb) on page 25 of the same cookbook.

Poached Perch

This terrific fish recipe does not leave your home smelling fishy when you are done cooking it, and I very much appreciate that.

12	ounces perch* (lake is best)	Juice of 1 lemon (about ¼ cup)
1	tablespoon minced dried chives	1 bay leaf
1	cup fat-free skim milk	1 teaspoon dried parsley

- Spray a 12-inch, nonstick skillet with nonfat cooking spray.
- Place the fish in the skillet and top with the chives, milk, and lemon juice.
- Place the bay leaf in the skillet in the milk.
- Cover and cook on medium-high heat for 8 to 10 minutes, or until the fish flakes in the center when tested with a fork.
- Sprinkle the cooked fish lightly with the parsley.
- Remove the fish with a slotted spoon and serve hot.
- Discard the fish broth.

Note: You can use other fish, such as cod and white fish.

Yield: 3 (4-ounce) servings

Calories: 118 (9% fat); Total Fat: 1 gm; Cholesterol: 105 mg; Carbohydrate: 3 gm; Dietary Fiber: 0 gm; Protein: 23 gm; Sodium: 81 mg
Diabetic Exchanges: 3 very lean meat

Preparation time: 5 minutes
Cooking time: 10 minutes
Total time: 15 minutes

Menu Idea: The Tomato Zing Salad on page 52 and the Sweet and Sour Bacon Salad Dressing on page 62 (both from *Busy People's Down-Home Cooking Without the Down-Home Fat*) taste superior on top of your favorite fresh lettuce salad.

Spicy Penne Rigate

This spicy entrée is oh-so-delicious for people who like fiery foods. Watch your taste buds sizzle as you enjoy every bite.

1 **(12-ounce) box reduced-carb penne pasta**	1 **tablespoon Worcestershire sauce**
1/2 **medium red bell pepper, finely chopped (about 3/4 cup)**	1 **tablespoon soy sauce**
	1 **(14.5-ounce) can diced tomatoes with green chilies (Do not drain.)**
1 **(12-ounce) bag sausage-flavored Ground Meatless***	1 **(8-ounce) bag fat-free shredded Cheddar cheese**

- Cook the pasta in boiling water as directed on the box.
- In a 12-inch, nonstick skillet cook the red bell pepper, Ground Meatless, Worcestershire sauce, soy sauce, tomatoes, and chilies for 5 to 6 minutes over medium heat or until the red bell pepper is tender.
- Stir in the cheese. Reduce the heat to medium-low, cover, and continue cooking for another 5 minutes, stirring occasionally until the cheese is completely melted.
- In a large bowl stir the sauce in with the cooked pasta.
- Serve hot.

*Note: Ground Meatless is a vegetarian meat substitute made by Morningstar Farms. It's found in the freezer section of your grocery store.

Yield: 9 (1-cup) servings

Calories: 236 (10% fat); Total Fat: 3 gm; Cholesterol: 5 mg; Carbohydrate: 35 gm; Dietary Fiber: 4 gm; Protein: 21 gm; Sodium: 810 mg
Diabetic Exchanges: 2 starch, 1 vegetable, 2 very lean meat

Preparation time: 5 minutes
Cooking time: 10 minutes or less
Total time: 15 minutes or less

Menu Idea: This feisty dish is complemented with side dishes that are cool and mild along with a refreshing, crisp green salad topped with my homemade Creamy Blue Cheese Salad Dressing (with only 4 carbs) on page 64 in *Busy People's Down-Home Cooking Without the Down-Home Fat.*

Salmon with Creamy Dill Sauce

I got this idea from an elaborate, expensive, hotel restaurant. As you can imagine, it was way overpriced. I honestly cannot tell the difference in flavor. I guarantee you one thing, if you purchase your salmon on sale, you can make about ten to twelve servings for less than the fancy, overpriced restaurant charges for one small serving.

2 pounds fresh salmon	1/4 cup fat-free mayonnaise
1/3 cup water	1/2 cup fat-free, low-carb milk
1/4 cup fat-free whipped salad dressing	2 or more teaspoons dried dill

- Preheat the oven to 400 degrees. (Or preheat a grill to medium hot.)
- Line a baking sheet with aluminum foil. Spray the foil with nonfat cooking spray. (Lemon-flavored cooking spray tastes wonderful.)
- Place the fish with skin side down on the prepared foil.
- Pour the water down the center of the fish.
- Fold the aluminum foil securely closed. If needed, use another piece of foil for the top and fold the edges of the top and bottom layers of foil together. The juices from the fish will steam-cook the fish.
- Cook in the oven on the center rack (or on the grill) for 10 to 15 minutes or until the salmon flakes easily when tested with a fork in the center. (Allow about 12 minutes per 1-inch thickness.)
- While the fish is baking, in a microwaveable bowl stir together the salad dressing, mayonnaise, milk, and dill until well blended.
- Once the fish is fully cooked, microwave the dill sauce for 30 seconds or until fully heated.
- Remove the salmon from the foil and place it on a serving platter, or cut the fish into eight servings and put them on individual plates.
- Spoon 2 tablespoons of the creamy dill sauce on each 4-ounce serving of cooked salmon.

Yield: 8 servings (4 ounces salmon and 2 tablespoons sauce)

Calories: 169 (36% fat); Total Fat: 6 gm; Cholesterol: 62 mg; Carbohydrate: 2 gm; Dietary Fiber: 0 gm; Protein: 23 gm; Sodium: 210 mg
Diabetic Exchanges: 3 lean meat

Preparation time: 5 minutes or less
Cooking time: 15 minutes or less
Total time: 20 minutes or less

Menu Idea: This is such a special entrée that it deserves special side dishes as well, such as the Glazed Green Beans on page 107 in *Busy People's Slow Cooker Cookbook*. Finish the meal with a Soft Apple Cinnamon Cookie (with only 7 carbs) on page 236 in *Busy People's Diabetic Cookbook*.

Sesame Seed Citrus Chicken

The longer this chicken marinates, the better it tastes. To save time I'll even put this in a Ziploc bag and into the freezer so it'll be ready to cook when I'm ready. It can be marinating in the freezer for up to two months or in the refrigerator for up to two days. This is also terrific cooked on the grill.

1	cup sugar-free orange drink	8	(4-ounce) pieces skinless, boneless chicken
1	tablespoon light soy sauce	1	teaspoon sesame seeds

- Put the orange drink, soy sauce, and chicken into a Ziploc bag.
- Marinate for at least 10 minutes and up to 2 days, turning the bag over a couple of times to completely soak the chicken.

For the grill:
- Prepare a grill to medium-high heat and grill the chicken for 4 to 5 minutes per side, or until the chicken is completely white all the way through the center and there is no visible pink at all. When grilling, I recommend chicken that has been marinating in the freezer or the refrigerator for at least a day. Because grilled chicken is not being cooked in the marinade, it takes longer for the chicken to absorb the marinated flavors.

To bake:
- Preheat the oven to 400 degrees.
- Line a jelly-roll pan with foil. (A jelly-roll pan is a cookie sheet with a ½-inch lip around the edge to prevent juices or marinades from running off the pan.) Spray the foil with nonfat cooking spray.
- Bake the chicken in the marinade in the prepared pan for 8 minutes on a middle rack in the oven covered with aluminum foil.
- Remove the foil. Turn the chicken over. Continue baking the chicken on the middle rack for another 6 minutes or until the chicken is no longer pink in the center.
- Turn the oven to broil.
- Sprinkle the top of the chicken with the sesame seeds and broil about 3 inches away from the heat source for 3 minutes or until the seeds are golden brown.
- Serve hot.

Variations: You can easily substitute sirloin steak or pork tenderloin for the chicken.

Yield: 8 (4-ounce) servings

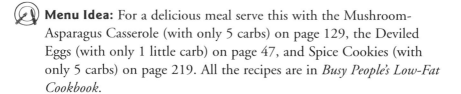

(with chicken) Calories: 129 (12% fat); Total Fat: 2 gm; Cholesterol: 66 mg; Carbohydrate: 0 gm; Dietary Fiber: 0 gm; Protein: 26 gm; Sodium: 188 mg Diabetic Exchanges: 3 very lean meat
(with steak) Calories: 155 (34% fat); Total Fat: 6 gm; Cholesterol: 71 mg; Carbohydrate: 0 gm; Dietary Fiber: 0 gm; Protein: 24 gm; Sodium: 167 mg Diabetic Exchanges: 3 lean meat
(with pork) Calories: 140 (28% fat); Total Fat: 4 gm; Cholesterol: 74 mg; Carbohydrate: 0 gm; Dietary Fiber: 0 gm; Protein: 24 gm; Sodium: 171 mg Diabetic Exchanges: 3 lean meat

Preparation time: 13 minutes
Cooking time: 17 minutes
Total time: 30 minutes

Menu Idea: For a delicious meal serve this with the Mushroom-Asparagus Casserole (with only 5 carbs) on page 129, the Deviled Eggs (with only 1 little carb) on page 47, and Spice Cookies (with only 5 carbs) on page 219. All the recipes are in *Busy People's Low-Fat Cookbook.*

Lemon-Garlic Chicken

The longer this marinates the better it tastes. If desired you can even freeze the chicken in the marinade for up to two months so it is ready when you want it.

8 (4-ounce) pieces skinless, boneless chicken	1/2 cup sugar-free lemonade
2 tablespoons minced garlic (from a jar)	1 tablespoon light soy sauce
	1 fresh lemon, cut into 8 wedges

- Preheat the oven to 400 degrees.
- Place the chicken between two pieces of wax paper and pound to 1/2-inch thickness.
- Put the garlic, lemonade, soy sauce, and chicken into a Ziploc bag and marinate at room temperature for at least 10 minutes (and up to 2 days in the refrigerator), turning the bag over a couple of times to completely soak the chicken.
- Line a jelly-roll pan with foil, and spray it with nonfat cooking spray.
- Place the chicken and the marinade in the prepared pan. Cover with aluminum foil and bake for 8 minutes. Turn chicken pieces over and bake 7 minutes on the other side or until it is no longer pink in the center.
- Serve hot garnished with a lemon wedge on top of each serving.

Yield: 8 (4-ounce) servings

Calories: 130 (10% fat); Total Fat: 1 gm; Cholesterol: 66 mg; Carbohydrate: 1 gm;
Dietary Fiber: 0 gm; Protein: 26 gm; Sodium: 189 mg
Diabetic Exchanges: 3 very lean meat

Preparation time: 15 minutes
Cooking time: 15 minutes
Total time: 30 minutes

Menu Idea: An asset to this chicken dinner would be a salad of freshly tossed, assorted lettuce topped with the Cool & Creamy Salsa Salad Dressing (with only 3 carbs) on page 63 in *Busy People's Down-Home Cooking Without the Down-Home Fat.*

Vermont-Inspired Barbeque Shredded Chicken

The marvelous maple flavor Vermont is well known for inspired this recipe. We traveled through Vermont in 1984, and the wonderful maple aroma and flavor captured my taste buds. To this day, my mouth still begins to water every time I think of it.

1/2 cup ketchup	1/4 to 1/2 teaspoon maple flavoring (found near vanilla extract)
1/3 cup Spenda Granular	
1/4 cup apple cider vinegar	2 (9.75-ounce) cans fat-free chicken breast, drained
2 teaspoons Worcestershire sauce	

- In a medium-size mixing bowl stir together the ketchup, Splenda, vinegar, Worcestershire sauce, maple flavoring, and chicken until well mixed.
- Heat in the microwave for 2 minutes. Stir, return to the microwave, and cook an additional 2 minutes.
- This is good served hot or chilled.

Yield: 9 to 10 (1/4-cup) servings

Calories: 81 (13% fat); Total Fat: 1 gm; Cholesterol: 26 mg; Carbohydrate: 5 gm; Dietary Fiber: 0 gm; Protein: 12 gm; Sodium: 400 mg
Diabetic Exchanges: 1/2 other carbohydrate, 1 1/2 very lean meat

Preparation time: 7 minutes or less

Menu Idea: A serving of this with celery sticks or chilled on a salad is good for a light lunch with the Fruit Casseroles recipe in this book on page 247 as a side dish. I also like it as an appetizer spread on low-carb crackers.

Tex-Mex Chicken

Now you can enjoy a southwestern meal without being concerned with how many carbohydrates are in it.

8	(4-ounce) pieces skinless, boneless chicken	4	teaspoons dried chives or 8 teaspoons chopped fresh chives
1	teaspoon ground cumin	8	teaspoons fat-free sour cream
2	cups salsa, drained		Paprika (optional)
1	cup fat-free shredded Cheddar cheese		

- Preheat the oven to 375 degrees.
- Spray a jelly-roll pan (cookie sheet with a ½-inch lip around the edge) with nonfat cooking spray.
- Pound each chicken piece between two sheets of wax paper to ½-inch thickness and place on the prepared jelly-roll pan.
- Sprinkle each piece of chicken with ⅛ teaspoon ground cumin.
- Cover with foil and bake in the preheated oven for 5 minutes.
- Turn the chicken over and spread ¼ cup salsa, 2 tablespoons cheese, and ½ teaspoon chives on each piece.
- Replace the foil, making sure the foil does not touch the cheese, and bake an additional 7 to 8 minutes or until the chicken is fully cooked and white in center. There should be no pink.
- Top each serving of chicken with 1 teaspoon sour cream, and then sprinkle lightly with paprika if desired.

Yield: 8 servings

Calories: 172 (9% fat); Total Fat: 1 gm; Cholesterol: 69 mg; Carbohydrate: 4 gm; Dietary Fiber: 0 gm; Protein: 31 gm; Sodium: 493 mg
Diabetic Exchanges: 4 very lean meat

Preparation time: 10 minutes
Cooking time: 20 minutes or less
Total time: 30 minutes or less

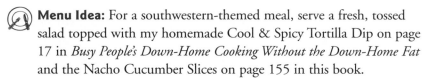

Menu Idea: For a southwestern-themed meal, serve a fresh, tossed salad topped with my homemade Cool & Spicy Tortilla Dip on page 17 in *Busy People's Down-Home Cooking Without the Down-Home Fat* and the Nacho Cucumber Slices on page 155 in this book.

Caribbean Chicken

I was pleasantly surprised by the flavor just this little bit of coconut added to this dish. Not only was it good cooked in the skillet, it was just as good on the grill.

4	(4-ounce) pieces boneless, skinless chicken, all fat removed	1/4	cup soy sauce
1	cup sugar-free lemonade	1/2	tablespoon shredded coconut
		1	tablespoon cornstarch

- Put the chicken, lemonade, soy sauce, and coconut in a Ziploc bag and marinate for 15 minutes, turning the bag over after 7 minutes.
- Cook the chicken in a skillet over medium-low heat until done, about 15 minutes.
- While the chicken is cooking, briskly whisk the marinade in a saucepan, stirring the cornstarch into the cold marinade until the cornstarch is dissolved.
- Turn the heat to medium. Stir and cook until the marinade becomes a thick sauce for dipping the chicken. Serve the sauce on the side.

Yield: 4 servings (4 ounces chicken and 1 tablespoon sauce)

Calories: 147 (11% fat); Total Fat: 2 gm; Cholesterol: 66 mg; Carbohydrate: 4 gm;
Dietary Fiber: 0 gm; Protein: 27 gm; Sodium: 993 mg
Diabetic Exchanges: 3 very lean meat

Preparation time: 15 minutes
Cooking time: 15 minutes or less
Total time: 30 minutes or less

Menu Idea: The Tropical Cabbage (with 15 carbs) on page 80 in *Busy People's Slow Cooker Cookbook* along with a fresh garden salad topped with my Sweet & Sour Bacon Salad Dressing (with only 3 carbs) on page 62 of *Busy People's Down-Home Cooking Without the Down-Home Fat* will be good to start your meal off.

Teriyaki Chicken

I was concerned that I wouldn't be able to capture the wonderful flavors I love in traditional teriyaki sauces without using the high-carb pineapple juice I like so much. I was amazed at how delicious this is. So were my dinner guests.

1/2 cup soy sauce	1/2 teaspoon garlic powder
1/2 cup red wine vinegar	8 (4-ounce) pieces skinless, boneless chicken, all fat removed
1/2 cup Splenda Granular, measures like sugar	
1 teaspoon ground ginger	1/8 cup cornstarch

- Put soy sauce, red wine vinegar, Splenda, ginger, and garlic powder into a Ziploc bag, seal it closed, and shake until well blended.
- Add the chicken and marinate at least 20 minutes or marinate ahead of time in the freezer until ready to cook.
- Prepare a grill to medium-low heat and grill for 4 to 5 minutes with lid of the grill closed.
- While the chicken is grilling, pour the marinade into a skillet over medium-low heat. Whisk in the cornstarch and continue whisking until thick, about 2 minutes. Make sure your marinade is cold before you add the cornstarch, otherwise the sauce will be lumpy.
- Once the sauce is thick, turn the chicken over, and spread the sauce on the top of the chicken. Continue cooking for another 4 to 5 minutes or until the chicken is white in the center and there is no pink.

Yield: 8 (4-ounce) servings

Calories: 148 (9% fat); Total Fat: 1 gm; Cholesterol: 66 mg; Carbohydrate: 5 gm;
Dietary Fiber: 0 gm; Protein: 27 gm; Sodium: 988 mg
Diabetic Exchanges: $^{1}/_{2}$ other carbohydrate, 3 very lean meat

Preparation time: 20 minutes or less
Cooking time: 10 minutes or less
Total time: 30 minutes or less

Menu Idea: This chicken tastes wonderful with a fresh garden salad
topped with my Sweet & Sour Bacon Salad Dressing (with only
3 carbs per serving) on page 62 in *Busy People's Down-Home Cooking
Without the Down-Home Fat.* Serve along with Deviled Eggs (with
only 1 carb) on page 47 in *Busy People's Low-Fat Cookbook.*

Sweet Onion Marinated Chicken

This recipe is one of the juiciest chicken entrées I have ever eaten. You are going to love it. For the best flavor let the chicken marinate for a day or two in the refrigerator.

³/4 cup finely chopped sweet onion (Vidalia onions are excellent)	¹/4 cup ketchup
¹/2 cup water	¹/3 cup red wine vinegar
¹/3 cup Splenda Granular, measures like sugar	1 tablespoon Worcestershire sauce
	8 (4-ounce) pieces skinless, boneless chicken

- In a Ziploc bag mix together the onion, water, Splenda, ketchup, vinegar, and Worcestershire sauce.
- With a fork, pierce the chicken all over and marinate for at least 20 minutes.
- Heat a grill to medium-low and cook the chicken for 4 to 5 minutes. Turn and cook an additional 4 to 5 minutes or until the chicken is no longer pink in the center.
- Serve hot.

Note: Boil the marinade for 2 minutes and serve on the side as a dipping sauce. *Do not use the marinade, though, if you do not cook it first.*

Yield: 8 (4-ounce) servings

Calories: 137 (10% fat); Total Fat: 1 gm; Cholesterol: 66 mg; Carbohydrate: 3 gm; Dietary Fiber: 0 gm; Protein: 26 gm; Sodium: 178 mg
Diabetic Exchanges: 3 very lean meat

Preparation time: 5 minutes
Cooking time: 10 minutes
Total time: 15 minutes

Menu Idea: The Sesame Seed Coleslaw recipe on page 126 in this book and the Cheese Ball (spread in celery sticks, with only 6 carbohydrates) on page 20 in *Busy People's Down-Home Cooking Without the Down-Home Fat* make a meal everyone will enjoy.

Garlic Parmesan Chicken

This great recipe is super anytime of the year.

8 (4-ounce) pieces skinless, boneless chicken	3/4 cup finely shredded Parmesan cheese (not grated)
3 tablespoons minced garlic (from a jar)	1 teaspoon dried parsley
2 teaspoons garlic salt	

- Preheat the oven to 350 degrees.
- Spray a jelly-roll pan (cookie sheet with ½-inch edge) with nonfat cooking spray.
- Put the chicken between two pieces of wax paper, and pound with a rolling pin or the side of a can to flatten to ¼-inch thickness. Place on the prepared jelly-roll pan.
- Spread 1 teaspoon minced garlic on one side of each piece of chicken.
- Sprinkle each piece of chicken lightly with ¼ teaspoon garlic salt.
- Cover with foil and bake for 5 minutes.
- Turn the chicken over. Sprinkle each piece of chicken with 1½ tablespoons Parmesan cheese and top with a pinch of parsley. Do not put the foil back on; discard the foil.
- Bake for an additional 5 to 7 minutes or until chicken is no longer pink in the center. Serve hot.

Yield: 8 (4-ounce) servings

Calories: 161 (20% fat); Total Fat: 3 gm; Cholesterol: 71 mg; Carbohydrate: 1 gm;
Dietary Fiber: 0 gm; Protein: 29 gm; Sodium: 442 mg
Diabetic Exchanges: 3½ very lean meat

Preparation time: 10 minutes
Cooking time: 15 minutes
Total time: 25 minutes

Menu Idea: The "Try-to Fool-'Em Angel Hair Pasta" recipe in this book on page 159 topped with your favorite low-carb spaghetti sauce and the Little Italy Tossed Salad on page 120 in this book completes a delicious, Italian-theme, low-carb meal without anyone missing the carbohydrates.

Mesquite Chicken Breasts with a Creamy Artichoke Sauce

The flavor combination is a winner and so is the ease of preparing this meal.

6 (3-ounce) mesquite-flavored precooked chicken breast fillets*	1 teaspoon ranch salad dressing mix (do not make as directed)
1 (14-ounce) can artichoke hearts, drained and hard part of hearts removed	1 (12-ounce) jar chicken gravy
	2 ounces fat-free cream cheese

- Heat the chicken, artichokes, dressing mix, gravy, and cream cheese in a 12-inch skillet on medium heat stirring occasionally. Keep covered in between stirrings.
- Once the cream cheese is completely melted and the meat is fully heated, reduce the heat to low.
- Simmer for 4 to 5 minutes.
- Serve hot.

Note: You should be able to find precooked chicken breasts in the freezer section of your local grocery store.

Yield: 6 (3-ounce) chicken breasts

Calories: 172 (29% fat); Total Fat: 5 gm; Cholesterol: 57 mg; Carbohydrate: 8 gm; Dietary Fiber: 0 gm; Protein: 23 gm; Sodium: 1059 mg
Diabetic Exchanges: 1½ vegetable, 3 lean meat

Preparation time: 5 minutes
Cooking time: 15 minutes or less
Total time: 20 minutes or less

Menu Idea: The California Medley Soup (with only 4 carbs) on page 70 and the Mushroom-Asparagus Casserole on page 129, both in *Busy People's Low-Fat Cookbook,* make this a superb meal.

Hawaiian Pizzas

You can use low-carb tortillas; however, we tested with both, and in this recipe we really think it tastes best with the low-fat versus the low-carb. The low-fat tortillas taste like a super-thin crispy pizza crust.

10 (10-inch) low-fat tortillas	1/2 cup chopped green onion
1/2 cup Teriyaki Baste and Glaze Sauce (I use Kikkoman's.)	1 (8-ounce) bag extra-lean ham, chopped
1 (8-ounce) bag fat-free mozzarella cheese	
1 (5.5-ounce) can pineapple tidbits in their own juice, drained and juice discarded	

- Preheat the oven to 400 degrees.
- Spray the bottoms of the tortillas with nonfat cooking spray.
- Spread 2 teaspoons Teriyaki Baste and Glaze Sauce over each tortilla.
- Lightly sprinkle 1 heaping tablespoon cheese evenly over each pizza.
- Top the pizzas with 1½ tablespoons pineapple, 1 teaspoon green onion, and 1 tablespoon ham.
- Put each tortilla pizza directly on the rack in the oven.
- Bake for 7 minutes or until the cheese is melted.
- Serve hot.

Yield: 10 (10-inch) pizzas (1 pizza per serving)

Calories: 257 (6% fat); Total Fat: 2 gm; Cholesterol: 16 mg; Carbohydrate: 41 gm; Dietary Fiber: 4 gm; Protein: 18 gm; Sodium: 1334 mg
Diabetic Exchanges: 2 starch, 1 other carbohydrate, 2 very lean meat

Preparation time: 10 minutes
Cooking time: 7 minutes
Total time: 17 minutes

Menu Idea: This is one of my favorite pizzas served with the fresh Red Lettuce Salad, on page 113 of this book.

Barbequed Chicken Pizza

These pizzas are great to put together in a jiffy for a meal that's tasty and cost effective. (Hey! I'd call that fast, smart, and thrifty.)

10 (10-inch) low-carb tortillas	1/2 cup chopped onion
1/2 cup barbeque sauce	4 ounces fresh sliced mushrooms
1 (12-ounce) can chicken breast, drained	1 medium red pepper, chopped (about 1 cup)
1 (8-ounce) bag fat-free, shredded Cheddar cheese	

- Preheat the oven to 400 degrees.
- Spray cookie sheets with nonfat cooking spray.
- Spray the bottoms of the tortillas with nonfat cooking spray. Place the tortillas on the cookie sheets, not touching each other.
- Stir the barbeque sauce and chicken together until well mixed.
- Spread 1 rounded tablespoon of the barbequed chicken mixture on each tortilla.
- Sprinkle the cheese evenly over all the pizzas lightly.
- Top the pizzas with onion, mushrooms, and red pepper.
- Bake for 5 to 7 minutes or until the cheese is melted.
- Serve hot.

Yield: 10 (10-inch) pizzas (1 pizza per serving)

Calories: 201 (22% fat); Total Fat: 5 gm; Cholesterol: 19 mg; Carbohydrate: 21 gm; Dietary Fiber: 5 gm; Protein: 21 gm; Sodium: 663 mg
Diabetic Exchanges: 1 starch, 1/2 other carbohydrate, 2 1/2 lean meat

Preparation time: 10 minutes or less
Cooking time: 7 minutes or less
Total time: 17 minutes or less

Menu Idea: The Red Wine Vinaigrette Cucumber Salad (with only 5 carbs) on page 49 of *Busy People's Down-Home Cooking Without the Down-Home Fat* is an excellent side salad for these pizzas instead of the traditional tossed salad.

Sausage & Sauerkraut Casserole

Zesty and full of flavor, this dish satisfies the taste buds' desire for ample, robust flavors.

(16-ounce) bag frozen crinkle-cut carrots	(32-ounce) jar sauerkraut, rinsed and squeezed dry
(12-ounce) bag sausage-flavored Ground Meatless*	(8-ounce) package fat-free shredded mozzarella cheese

- Cook the carrots in the microwave for 3 to 4 minutes, or until tender, to help precook the carrots.
- Spray a nonstick, 12-inch skillet with nonfat cooking spray.
- Over medium heat cook the Ground Meatless and sauerkraut until fully heated. Cover and stir occasionally.
- The carrots will finish cooking in the microwave in the meantime. Stir them into the skillet with the sausage and sauerkraut.
- Once the entire dish is fully heated, sprinkle it with the cheese. Cover with a lid. Reduce the heat to low. Let sit for 1 to 2 minutes or until the cheese is melted.
- Serve hot.

Note: Ground Meatless is a vegetarian meat substitute made by Morningstar Farms. It's found in the freezer section of your grocery store. If desired, you can use cooked and crumbled turkey Italian sausage instead, but the nutritional information will be different.

Yield: 6 servings

Calories: 190 (4% fat); Total Fat: 1 gm; Cholesterol: 7 mg; Carbohydrate: 20 gm; Dietary Fiber: 9 gm; Protein: 26 gm; Sodium: 1789 mg
Diabetic Exchanges: $1/2$ starch, 2 vegetable, 3 very lean meat

Preparation time: 5 minutes or less
Cooking time: 10 minutes or less
Total time: 15 minutes or less

Menu Idea: Serve with the Red Lettuce Salad recipe on page 113 in this book topped with your favorite low-carb salad dressing.

Bacon & Cheese Egg Melt

A home-cooked breakfast loaded with lean protein couldn't be any easier to prepare. It's the answer to wanting a hot breakfast fast.

¼ cup liquid egg substitute	1 tablespoon fat-free shredded Cheddar cheese
1 slice Canadian bacon	

- Spray a microwave-safe cereal bowl with nonfat cooking spray.
- Put the egg substitute into the prepared bowl.
- Microwave for 30 seconds.
- Place the Canadian bacon on top of the egg.
- Sprinkle the cheese on top of the bacon.
- Cover with wax paper.
- Microwave for another 30 seconds or until the cheese is melted and the egg is fully cooked.
- With a spatula, slide the Bacon and Cheese Egg Melt out of the bowl onto a serving plate.

Yield: 1 serving

Calories: 65 (11% fat); Total Fat: 1 gm; Cholesterol: 14 mg; Carbohydrate: 1 gm; Dietary Fiber: 0 gm; Protein: 12 gm; Sodium: 503 mg
Diabetic Exchanges: 2 very lean meat

Preparation time: 3 minutes or less
Cooking time: 1 minute
Total time: 4 minutes or less

Menu Idea: Many of the beverages in this cookbook are a terrific complement to meals for a source of healthy carbohydrates as well as lean proteins. Some for breakfast that I suggest are Cold Cappuccino Frothy on page 42, Cinnamon & Spice Coffee on page 40, the Tomato Juice Cooler on page 33, or the Banana-Blueberry Milkshake on page 25, all in this book.

Spicy Italian Cabbage Dinner

This reminds me of the insides of a spicy Chinese egg roll. If you like the insides of egg rolls, you're going to love this.

1 (16-ounce) package precut coleslaw (found in produce section)	4 ounces fresh mushrooms, thinly sliced
1/2 cup water	1/2 teaspoon ground cinnamon
1 (12-ounce) package sausage-flavored Ground Meatless*	1 teaspoon Splenda Granular, measures like sugar
	2 tablespoons fat-free French salad dressing

- Spray a slow cooker with nonfat cooking spray.
- In the slow cooker stir together the coleslaw, water, sausage, and mushrooms until well mixed.
- Cover and cook on high for 1½ to 2 hours or on low for 3 to 4 hours.
- Stir into the cooked cabbage mixture the cinnamon, Splenda, and salad dressing until well mixed.
- Serve hot.

Note: Ground Meatless is a vegetarian meat substitute made by Morningstar Farms. It tastes just as good, but without all the fat. It's found in the freezer section of your grocery store.

Yield: 4 (1¼-cup) servings

Calories: 157 (0% fat); Total Fat: 0 gm; Cholesterol: 0 mg; Carbohydrate: 18 gm; Dietary Fiber: 8 gm; Protein: 20 gm; Sodium: 408 mg
Diabetic Exchanges: ½ starch, 2 vegetable, 2 very lean meat

Preparation time: 5 minutes or less

Menu Idea: From *Busy Peoples Diabetic Cookbook* try such low-carb desserts as Coconut Cookies (with 7 carbs) on page 246, Chocolate Sour Cream Cookies (with 6 carbs) on page 236, or Very Vanilla Cookies (with 7 carbs) on page 239.

Cabbage Lasagna

This is a terrific substitute for high-carbohydrate and higher-calorie lasagna pasta. It has a superb flavor and texture.

2 (8-ounce) packages shredded fat-free mozzarella cheese	9 large cabbage leaves*
1 (26.5-ounce) jar fat-free, low-carb spaghetti sauce	½ cup liquid egg substitute
1 (12-ounce) package sausage-flavored Ground Meatless**	1 (16-ounce) container fat-free cottage cheese

- Spray a slow cooker with nonfat cooking spray.
- Set aside 1 cup mozzarella cheese to top the lasagna near the end of cooking time.
- Put ½ cup spaghetti sauce in the bottom of the slow cooker. Sprinkle with the Ground Meatless.
- Arrange 3 cabbage leaves on top.
- In a blender briefly mix the egg, cottage cheese, and 1½ packages of mozzarella cheese together for about 30 seconds.
- Spread one-third of the cheese mixture over the leaves.
- Top with one-third of the remaining sauce and one-third of the remaining meat.
- Repeat layering the cabbage, cheese mixture, sauce, and meat until all ingredients are used except the remaining reserved mozzarella cheese.
- Cover and cook on low for 6 hours or on high for 3 hours.
- Top with the reserved mozzarella cheese. Cover and cook for another 5 to 10 minutes, or until the cheese is melted.
- Cut into 12 servings and serve hot.

Note: Freezing the entire head of cabbage makes separating the leaves much easier.

**Ground Meatless is a vegetarian meat substitute made by Morningstar Farms. It's found in the freezer section of your grocery store. If desired, you can use cooked and crumbled turkey Italian sausage instead, but the nutritional information will be different.

Yield: 12 servings

Calories: 195 (21% fat); Total Fat: 4 gm; Cholesterol: 40 mg; Carbohydrate: 12 gm; Dietary Fiber: 4 gm; Protein: 25 gm; Sodium: 1057 mg
Diabetic Exchanges: 3 lean meat, 2 vegetable

Preparation time: 20 minutes or less

Menu Idea: In *Busy People's Down-Home Cooking Without the Down-Home Fat* there's a terrific Italian Broccoli recipe with only 5 carbs per serving on page 74 that's a great Italian-style side dish with this entrée.

Italian Burrito

This serving size is just right for a lunch or dinner. For people who like instant gratification, the temptation to overeat is a lot less tempting when we have to wait for another burrito to cook.

2 tablespoons pizza sauce	2 tablespoons sausage-flavored Ground Meatless*
1 (8-inch) low-carb flour tortilla	
1/4 cup fat-free shredded mozzarella cheese	1 teaspoon grated Parmesan cheese

- Spread the pizza sauce on the tortilla.
- Sprinkle the mozzarella cheese over the sauce.
- Arrange the Ground Meatless on top of the cheese.
- Sprinkle with the Parmesan cheese.
- Microwave for 20 to 45 seconds, or until the mozzarella cheese is completely melted.
- Roll-up the tortilla burrito style and serve hot.

Note: Ground Meatless is a vegetarian meat substitute made by Morningstar Farms. It's found in the freezer section of your grocery store. If desired, you can use cooked and crumbled turkey Italian sausage instead, but the nutritional information will be different.

Yield: 1 serving

Calories: 179 (26% fat); Total Fat: 6 gm; Cholesterol: 6 mg; Carbohydrate: 18 gm; Dietary Fiber: 7 gm; Protein: 18 gm; Sodium: 850 mg
Diabetic Exchanges: 1 starch, 2 lean meat

Preparation time: 5 minutes or less
Cooking time: 2 minutes or less
Total time: 7 minutes or less

Menu Idea: Red Lettuce Salad on page 113 in this book with fat-free Italian salad dressing makes this a great meal. The Crunchy Cucumbers with Cream on page 82 in *Busy People's Low-Fat Cookbook* is also a great side salad for this delicious Italian burrito sandwich.

Polynesian-Inspired Sloppy Joes

The unique flavors of the Polynesian Islands with its pineapple and the Teriyaki Baste & Glaze make this original recipe super for Hawaiian-theme parties.

1 pound ground eye of round	1/4 cup Teriyaki Baste and Glaze
1/2 cup chopped onion (fresh or frozen)	(I use Kikkoman's found near barbeque sauce)
1 (12-ounce) bag Ground Meatless*	2 tablespoons dried chives or 1/4 cup chopped fresh chives
1 (3-ounce) can crushed pineapple, drained, and juice discarded	

- In a 12-inch, nonstick skillet brown the eye of round over medium-high heat with the onion, stirring frequently. Rinse and drain any juices.
- Add the Ground Meatless, pineapple, Teriyaki Baste and Glaze, and chives.
- Continue cooking until fully heated.
- Serve in lettuce leaves or low-carb bread.

Note: Ground Meatless is a vegetarian meat substitute made by Morningstar Farms. It tastes just as good, but without all the fat. It's found in the freezer section of your grocery store.

Yield: 16 ($\frac{1}{4}$-cup) servings

(without bread) Calories: 72 (20% fat); Total Fat: 2 gm; Cholesterol: 16 mg; Carbohydrate: 4 gm; Dietary Fiber: 0 gm; Protein: 10 gm; Sodium: 225 mg Diabetic Exchanges: $1\frac{1}{2}$ very lean meat

Preparation time: 3 minutes
Cooking time: 10 minutes or less
Total time: 13 minutes or less

Menu Idea: I like this wrapped in lettuce leaves, because I like the crunchiness the crisp leaves add. As a meal with these I had the Cherry Slushies (with only 3 carbs) on page 200 and the Tomato Zing Salad (with 6 carbs) on page 52, both from *Busy People's Down-Home Cooking Without the Down-Home Fat.*

Taco Lettuce Wraps

This idea came from H. Dale Burke, a pastor in California who lost forty pounds switching to a lower carbohydrate lifestyle. His lovely wife lost twenty.

1 pound ground eye of round	1/2 cup fat-free, shredded Cheddar cheese (about 2 ounces)
1 (1.25-ounce) package taco seasoning	1/2 cup finely chopped tomato (about 1/2 medium tomato)
3/4 cup water	1/2 cup fat-free sour cream
8 large romaine lettuce leaves, cleaned	

- In a 12-inch nonstick skillet cook and crumble the ground beef. Rinse and drain the meat if needed.
- Add the taco seasoning mix and the water. Bring to a boil. Reduce the heat to low and simmer for 15 minutes, stirring occasionally.
- Put 2 tablespoons cooked taco meat inside each large lettuce leaf.
- Top the taco meat with 1 tablespoon cheese, 1 tablespoon chopped tomato, and 1 tablespoon sour cream.
- Fold each lettuce leaf as you would a soft taco.
- Eat immediately. (If desired, serve taco sauce on the side.)

Note: For an added special flavor, add 1/2 teaspoon ground cinnamon when you stir in the taco seasoning mix.

Yield: 4 (2-taco) servings

Calories: 241 (23% fat); Total Fat: 6 gm; Cholesterol: 70 mg; Carbohydrate: 14 gm; Dietary Fiber: 1 gm; Protein: 31 gm; Sodium: 778 mg
Diabetic Exchanges: 1 other carbohydrate, 4 lean meat

Preparation time: 10 minutes
Cooking time: 15 minutes
Total time: 25 minutes

Menu Idea: I like these tacos with the Fruit Punch recipe on page 202 of *Busy People's Down-Home Cooking Without the Down-Home Fat;* the punch has only 4 carbohydrates.

Ranch Hand Roll-Ups

This is a great wrapped sandwich for lunches.

1 tablespoon sour cream	2 tablespoons shredded fat-free Cheddar cheese
1/4 teaspoon ranch salad dressing mix (do not make as directed)	1 ounce deli-style, thinly sliced roast beef (about 1/4 cup)
1/4 teaspoon dried chives	
1 (6-inch) low-carb, soft-flour tortilla	

- In a small bowl mix the sour cream with the salad dressing mix and chives.
- Spread the dressing mix on the tortilla.
- Sprinkle the cheese on top.
- Press the meat onto the tortilla and microwave for 30 seconds.
- Roll up tightly and serve hot.

Yield: 1 rolled sandwich

Calories: 172 (26% fat); Total Fat: 5 gm; Cholesterol: 21 mg; Carbohydrate: 17 gm; Dietary Fiber: 5 gm; Protein: 17 gm; Sodium: 752 mg
Diabetic Exchanges: 1 starch, 2 lean meat

Preparation time: 5 minutes

Menu Idea: This is great with celery sticks and fresh cucumber slices with Bacon & Blue Cheese Dressing on page 149 in *Busy People's Diabetic Cookbook.*

Broccoli, Ham & Cheddar Pies

This is a very fancy looking entrée, and definitely a showstopper when a guest sees it for the first time. It is very impressive visually and tastes every bit as good as it looks. It is great for any meal.

1 (16-ounce) box phyllo (filo) dough, cut in half lengthwise	1 (10-ounce) package frozen chopped broccoli, thawed and squeezed dry
2 (8-ounce) containers liquid egg substitute (2 cups)	1 (8-ounce) package fat-free shredded Cheddar cheese
1 (1.4-ounce) package vegetable soup mix (do not make as directed)	1 (8-ounce) package extra-lean ham, chopped (about 1 cup)
1 cup low-fat ricotta cheese	

- Preheat the oven to 350 degrees.
- Spray two 9-inch springform pans (or pie plates) with nonfat cooking spray.
- Spray each strip of dough, one at a time, with nonfat cooking spray.
- Lay each strip across the entire pan, allowing the strips of dough to overlap each other and hang off the side. Gently press the strips of dough into the pans, arranging them like the spokes of a wheel. The dough will rip and wrinkle, but that's okay as long as the strips are overlapping. Use 20 strips per pan or pie plate.
- In a mixing bowl stir together the egg substitute, ricotta cheese, and soup mix until well blended.
- With your hands, squeeze as much moisture as possible from the broccoli. To the egg mixure, add the broccoli, cheddar cheese, and ham. Stir until well mixed.
- Put 1¾ cups egg mixture into each prepared pan.
- Fold the dough hanging over the edges in toward the center of the pans. Once all the sides are folded in and overlapping each other, spray the top with nonfat cooking spray in order to help the layers seal together.
- Bake for 20 minutes or until a knife inserted in the center comes out clean.
- Let sit for 10 minutes before cutting and serving. Cut each pie into 8 servings.

Note: If using pie plates bake 10 to 15 minutes longer.

Yield: 16 servings (8 servings per pie)

Calories: 173 (13% fat); Total Fat: 2 gm; Cholesterol: 14 mg; Carbohydrate: 23 gm;
Dietary Fiber: 1 gm; Protein: 14 gm; Sodium: 631 mg
Diabetic Exchanges: 1$\frac{1}{2}$ starch, 1$\frac{1}{2}$ very lean meat

Preparation time: 10 minutes
Cooking time: 20 minutes
Total time: 30 minutes

Menu Ideas: For breakfast or brunch I serve Mint Tea on page 208 in *Busy People's Down-Home Cooking Without the Down-Home Fat.* For lunch or dinner I serve Red Lettuce Salad on page 113 of this book along with a cup of California Medley Soup (with only 4 carbs) on page 70 of *Busy People's Low-Fat Cookbook.*

Ham & Spinach Turnovers

These fabulous turnovers are marvelous for a ladies' tea, breakfast, brunch, lunch, or dinner. They are light, crispy, and oh-so-delicious, yet filling and satisfying.

1 (10-ounce) package frozen spinach, thawed, drained, and chopped	1 (1.4-ounce) package vegetable soup mix (do not make as directed)
1 cup fat-free cottage cheese	10 sheets phyllo (filo) dough (half of a 16-ounce box)
1 (8-ounce) container liquid egg substitute	2 cups fat-free sour cream (optional)
1 (8-ounce) package extra-lean ham, finely chopped (about 1 cup)	

- Preheat the oven to 375 degrees.
- Spray four large cookie sheets with nonfat cooking spray.
- Stir the spinach, cottage cheese, egg substitute, ham, and soup mix together until well mixed.
- Cut the phyllo dough sheets into thirds lengthwise.
- Use only one strip of phyllo dough per turnover (⅓ of a sheet).
- Spray one side of the strip with nonfat cooking spray.
- Put ⅛ cup spinach mixture ½ inch away from the edge of the far left corner of each strip of phyllo dough.
- Fold each phyllo dough strip over the spinach mixture to form a triangle and keep folding all the way down the strip of dough.
- Spray the outside of the turnovers with nonfat cooking spray and place on the cookie sheet.
- Bake for 8 minutes or until the turnovers are crispy.
- Let sit a few minutes before eating; otherwise they will burn the top of your mouth.
- If desired, top each one with 1 teaspoon fat-free sour cream.

Note: It is very important that these are eaten within an hour or so, because they lose their crispiness and texture if they sit out too long or are stored. It is okay to make the spinach filling ahead of time.

Yield: 10 entrée servings (3 per serving)

Calories: 155 (14% fat); Total Fat: 2 gm; Cholesterol: 13 mg; Carbohydrate: 20 gm; Dietary Fiber: 2 gm; Protein: 13 gm; Sodium: 714 mg
Diabetic Exchanges: 1 starch, 1 vegetable, 1$\frac{1}{2}$ very lean meat

Preparation time: 22 minutes
Cooking time: 8 minutes
Total time: 30 minutes or less

Menu Idea: Serve as a dinner or lunch with a salad such as a fresh, tossed green salad topped with Cool and Creamy Salsa Salad Dressing (with only 3 carbs) on page 63 or Creamy Blue Cheese Salad Dressing (with only 4 carbs) on page 64, both recipes in *Busy People's Down-Home Cooking Without the Down-Home Fat.*

Grilled Honey-Dijon Pork Steaks

There actually is no honey in this recipe, but the diners will never know because the sweetness will make them think there is.

¹/₂ cup mustard	8 (4-ounce) pork tenderloin
3 individual packets Splenda	steaks, all visible fat removed

- Spray the grill with nonfat cooking spray. Preheat the grill to high.
- Mix the mustard and Splenda together until well blended.
- Put the pork steaks on a hot grill. (The grill is hot enough when you cannot hold your hand over the heat for more than 2 seconds.) Grill on high with the grill lid closed for 5 minutes.
- Turn the steaks over. Spread 1½ teaspoons sweetened mustard evenly over each steak. Close the lid again. Cook another 5 minutes.
- Turn the steaks over again. Spread 1½ teaspoons sweetened mustard evenly over each steak again.
- Close the lid again. Cook another 5 to 8 minutes, or until the steaks are no longer pink in the center, but still juicy.
- Serve hot.

Yield: 8 (4-ounce) servings

Calories: 147 (27% fat); Total Fat: 4 gm; Cholesterol: 74 mg; Carbohydrate: 2 gm; Dietary Fiber: 0 gm; Protein: 24 gm; Sodium: 225 mg
Diabetic Exchanges: 3 lean meat

Preparation time: 5 minutes
Cooking time: 15 to 18 minutes
Total time: 23 minutes

Menu Idea: *Busy People's Diabetic Cookbook* has numerous side dishes and salads that'd go good with this pork, such as French-Style Simmered Green Beans on page 170, Roasted Portabella Mushroom Caps on page 173, and Cucumber Salad with Bacon & Blue Cheese on page 148.

Magnificent Marinated Pork Steaks

Add zest to your steaks without a lot of hard-to-find ingredients with this super simple marinade.

1 cup ketchup	4 (4-ounce) pork tenderloin steaks
1 individual packet Splenda	
¼ cup mustard	

- Put the ketchup, Splenda, and mustard in a Ziploc bag. Close tightly. Shake until the ingredients are well blended.
- Allow the pork steaks to marinate at least 15 to 20 minutes in the marinade before cooking.
- Cook the steaks on the grill at high heat for 5 minutes and baste with the marinade. Turn and cook the other side for 5 minutes or until desired degree of doneness. Serve hot.
- Discard the unused marinade.

Yield: 4 (4-ounce) servings

Calories: 153 (25% fat); Total Fat: 4 gm; Cholesterol: 75 mg; Carbohydrate: 4 gm; Dietary Fiber: 0 gm; Protein: 24 gm; Sodium: 266 mg
Diabetic Exchanges: 3 lean meat

Preparation time: 20 minutes
Cooking time: 10 minutes
Total time: 30 minutes

Menu Idea: Serve this with Bacon Green Beans (page 102) or Garlic Beans (page 106) in *Busy People's Slow-Cooker Cookbook* along with the Savory Zucchini on page 113 in this book.

Pork with Herb & Mushrooms in Light Gravy

This very tender meat melts in your mouth.

1	(10.5-ounce) can pork-flavored gravy
1	teaspoon dried thyme
8	ounces sliced fresh button mushrooms
1/2	tablespoon Worcestershire sauce
1/2	tablespoon dried chives or 1 tablespoon chopped fresh chives
2	pounds pork tenderloin, cut into bite-size pieces

- Stir the pork gravy, thyme, mushrooms, Worcestershire sauce, chives, and pork in the bottom of a slow cooker.
- Cook on high for 2 hours or on low for 6 to 7 hours.
- With a spoon, mix the mushroom gravy in the slow cooker until well blended.
- Serve hot.

Yield: 8 (⅔-cup) servings

Calories: 172 (34% fat); Total Fat: 6 gm; Cholesterol: 76 mg; Carbohydrate: 3 gm; Dietary Fiber: 1 gm; Protein: 25 gm; Sodium: 283 mg
Diabetic Exchanges: 3 lean meat

Preparation time: 5 minutes

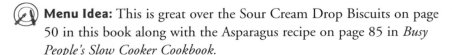 **Menu Idea:** This is great over the Sour Cream Drop Biscuits on page 50 in this book along with the Asparagus recipe on page 85 in *Busy People's Slow Cooker Cookbook.*

Salisbury Steak with Mushroom Gravy

Everyone in our family liked these so much they requested them again a few days later.

1 1/2 pounds ground eye of round	1 (12-ounce) jar beef-flavored gravy
1 plus 1 tablespoons Worcestershire sauce	8 ounces sliced fresh mushrooms
1/2 plus 1/2 cup chopped onion (fresh or frozen)	1/4 teaspoon dried thyme
1 teaspoon Mrs. Dash Salt-Free Original Seasoning Blend	

- Spray a 12-inch, nonstick skillet with nonfat cooking spray.
- In a medium-size mixing bowl mix together the beef, 1 tablespoon Worcestershire sauce, 1/2 cup chopped onion, and Mrs. Dash.
- Form the mixture into seven equal patties, using about 1/3 cup mixture for each patty, and cook the patties in the prepared skillet over medium-high heat for about 4 minutes with the lid on. While the meat is cooking, allow the remaining 1/2 cup onions to cook in the skillet beside the patties.
- Turn the patties over and cook another 3 to 4 minutes.
- Remove the cooked patties to a covered dish.
- Add the remaining 1 tablespoon Worcestershire sauce, gravy, mushrooms, and thyme to the skillet with the onions. Cover, reduce the heat to medium-low, and cook an additional 5 to 6 minutes or until the mushrooms are tender.
- Pour 1/4 cup gravy over each patty and serve hot.

Yield: 7 servings (1 patty and 3 ounces gravy)

Calories: 172 (32% fat); Total Fat: 6 gm; Cholesterol: 58 mg; Carbohydrate: 7 gm; Dietary Fiber: 1 gm; Protein: 23 gm; Sodium: 378 mg
Diabetic Exchanges: 1 1/2 vegetable, 3 lean meat

Preparation time: 6 minutes or less
Cooking time: 14 minutes
Total time: 20 minutes or less

Menu Idea: From this cookbook I suggest Cucumber, Dill & Tomato Salad (page 111) and the Zucchini & Onions for a side dish (page 154).

Meatballs in Savory Gravy

1/2 cup finely chopped onion	1 plus 1 tablespoons Worcestershire sauce
1/2 cup finely chopped green pepper (fresh or frozen)	1 tablespoon soy sauce
2 tablespoons water	1 (12-ounce) jar fat-free beef-flavored gravy
1 pound ground eye of round	

- In a 12-inch, nonstick skillet cook the onion and green pepper for about 5 minutes, covered, over medium heat.
- Put the cooked onion and green pepper in a bowl, and stir in the beef, 1 tablespoon Worcestershire sauce, and the soy sauce until well mixed.
- Form the mixture into 16 meatballs, about 1 rounded tablespoon per meatball.
- Cook the meatballs in the same skillet over medium heat for 5 to 6 minutes, turning occasionally. To quicken the cooking process put a lid on the skillet.
- Drain and discard the juices, move the beef balls to one side of the skillet, and on the empty side, stir the remaining 1 tablespoon Worcestershire sauce and gravy together until well blended. Gently coat the beef balls in the gravy.
- Turn the heat to low, cover, and let simmer for 2 to 3 minutes or until the gravy is fully heated. Serve hot.

Yield: 4 (4-meatball) servings

Calories: 195 (26% fat); Total Fat: 6 gm; Cholesterol: 70 mg; Carbohydrate: 11 gm; Dietary Fiber: 1 gm; Protein: 23 gm; Sodium: 810 mg
Diabetic Exchanges: 1/2 other carbohydrate, 3 lean meat

Preparation time: 15 minutes
Cooking time: 9 minutes
Total time: 24 minutes

Menu Idea: This is a versatile recipe. The beef balls are great as an appetizer, too, or as an entrée with the Asparagus & Mushrooms recipe (with only 6 carbs per serving) on page 70 in *Busy People's Down-Home Cooking Without the Down-Home Fat.*

Sirloin Steak with Feta Cream

My assistants and I knew we liked this, but I was pleasantly surprised at how very much my husband liked it. He had seconds at dinner and then again the next day requested it for his lunch.

2 teaspoons steak seasoning	2 tablespoons fat-free, low-carb milk
8 (4-ounce) boneless sirloin steak fillets, with all visible fat removed	1 plus 1 tablespoons finely chopped green onions
1/4 cup fat-free mayonnaise	1/4 cup fat-free sour cream
1/3 cup low-fat feta cheese crumbles	

- Preheat the grill to highest heat.
- Rub 1/4 teaspoon steak seasonings onto each of the steaks. Pound the steaks on both sides to help tenderize the meat and incorporate the steak seasoning. Place the steaks on the hot grill for 4 to 5 minutes.
- While the steaks are grilling, in a bowl stir together the mayonnaise, feta cheese, milk, 1 tablespoon green onion, and sour cream until well blended.
- Turn the steaks over. Put 1 tablespoon of the feta cream on each grilled steak.
- Close the grill lid again, and cook for 3 to 4 minutes for rare and up to 7 to 8 minutes for well done.
- Sprinkle the remaining green onion on top of the steaks before serving.
- Serve hot.

Yield: 8 servings (4-ounce steak and 1 tablespoon feta cream per serving)

Calories: 179 (33% fat); Total Fat: 6 gm; Cholesterol: 75 mg; Carbohydrate: 3 gm;
Dietary Fiber: 0 gm; Protein: 26 gm; Sodium: 375 mg
Diabetic Exchanges: $3\frac{1}{2}$ lean meat

Preparation time: 5 minutes
Cooking time: 13 minutes or less
Total time: 18 minutes or less

Menu Idea: From the *Busy People's Down-Home Cooking Without the Down-Home Fat* serve with the Portobello Garlic Mushrooms on page 13 and the Red Wine Vinaigrette Cucumber Salad on page 49.

Seconds, Please, London Broil

In this dish you marinate leftover steak after it has been cooked rather than prior to being cooked. I am very pleased with the mouth-watering results and was surprised at how it helps tenderize what would normally be thought of as dried, leftover steak.

I pound leftover grilled or cooked flank steak (also known as London broil)	2 tablespoons Teriyaki Baste and Glaze (I use Kikkoman's found with barbeque sauces)
1/2 cup sugar-free orange drink	

- Cut the flank steak diagonally into ⅓-inch strips.
- Put the orange drink and the Teriyaki Baste and Glaze in a Ziploc bag and marinate the steak in the refrigerator for at least 15 minutes and up to 2 days.
- When ready, heat the steak in the microwave for 15 to 30 seconds for each 4-ounce serving.

Variations: You can substitute leftover pork tenderloin or skinless, boneless chicken breast for the steak.

Yield: 4 (4-ounce) servings

Calories: 224 (35% fat); Total Fat: 8 gm; Cholesterol: 56 mg; Carbohydrate: 3 gm; Dietary Fiber: 0 gm; Protein: 32 gm; Sodium: 267 mg
Diabetic Exchanges: 4 lean meat

Preparation time: 15 minutes or less
Cooking time: 20 seconds or less per 4 ounce serving
Total time: 18 minutes or less

Menu Idea: This is great for a quick lunch the next day with a light salad from this cookbook, such as a serving of the Greek-Style Cucumber Salad on page 118.

European-Seasoned London Broil

This was a huge hit at one of my cookouts. I made more than enough so I could have leftovers, but our company ate every last bite and then kept saying, "Oh, I ate too much."

¹/₂ **teaspoon dried oregano**	1 **teaspoon dried parsley**
¹/₂ **teaspoon dried thyme**	¹/₂ **teaspoon horseradish**
¹/₂ **teaspoon onion powder**	1 **pound flank steak (London broil)**
¹/₂ **teaspoon garlic salt**	

- Preheat a grill to medium-high heat.
- Put the oregano, thyme, onion powder, garlic salt, parsley, and horseradish together in a small container with a lid. Shake until well mixed.
- Pound the steak on both sides diagonally across the grain for a total of about 2 minutes to tenderize it.
- Rub the seasonings onto both sides of the meat and grill for 4 to 5 minutes. Turn over and continue cooking another 3 to 4 minutes for medium to medium rare.
- With a very sharp knife, cut the steak into very thin slices diagonally across the grain of the meat.
- Serve immediately.

Yield: 4 (4-ounce) servings

Calories: 162 (36% fat); Total Fat: 6 gm; Cholesterol: 37 mg; Carbohydrate: 1 gm; Dietary Fiber: 0 gm; Protein: 25 gm; Sodium: 185 mg
Diabetic Exchanges: 3 lean meat

Preparation time: 5 minutes or less
Cooking time: 9 minutes or less
Total time: 14 minutes or less

Menu Idea: The Roasted Portabella Mushroom Caps (with only 3 carbs) on page 173 along with a Cherry Freeze drink (with only 7 carbs) on page 41, both in *Busy People's Diabetic Cookbook,* and Ranch Green Beans on page 151 of this book will round this off to a very nice dinner worth remembering.

Slow Cooker Stuffed Flank Steak

This flavorful steak tastes more like a roast when it's all done, and every bite melts in your mouth.

2 pounds flank steak (also known as London broil)	1 cup sliced fresh mushrooms
	1/4 cup dried parsley or 1/2 cup chopped fresh parsley
1 teaspoon steak seasoning blend (I use Tone's brand)	1 (10 3/4-ounce) can onion soup, not diluted
1 cup chopped onion	
3 tablespoons minced garlic	

- Pound the steak on both sides with either a meat mallet or the edge of a plate to help tenderize the beef.
- Sprinkle with the steak seasoning.
- Mix the onion, garlic, mushrooms, and parsley together until well mixed. Spread on the seasoned steak.
- Roll the steak lengthwise jelly roll style (starting at the longest side), and tie with string about every 2 inches.
- Place in a slow cooker. Pour the onion soup into the slow cooker.
- Cover and cook on low for 6 hours.
- Cut into 8 pieces and serve hot.

Yield: 8 (4-ounce) servings

Calories: 193 (32% fat); Total Fat: 7 gm; Cholesterol: 37 mg; Carbohydrate: 6 gm; Dietary Fiber: 1 gm; Protein: 26 gm; Sodium: 471 mg
Diabetic Exchanges: 3 lean meat, 1 vegetable

 Preparation time: 15 minutes

 Menu Idea: *Busy People's Diabetic Cookbook* has 71 low-carb recipes in it. Two recipes from the book that are superb with this entrée are the Wilted Fresh Spinach with Herbs on page 171 and the Roasted Portabella Mushroom Caps on page 173. Both only have 3 carbs each.

Slow Roasted Italian-Style London Broil

The meat is tenderized as it cooks by the tomatoes, and the entire entrée is flavorful throughout.

2 pounds flank steak (also known as London broil)	1½ tablespoons Italian seasoning
2 (14-ounce) cans diced tomatoes with chilies	½ teaspoon garlic salt
	1 medium onion, sliced

- Beat the steak with the edge of a plate to tenderize it.
- Stir the tomatoes, Italian seasoning, and garlic salt in a slow cooker until well mixed.
- Submerge the steak into the tomatoes.
- Place the onion on top.
- Cover and cook on low for 6 to 7 hours or on high for 3 hours.
- Cut the steak into thin strips across the grain.
- Serve with gravy on the side.

Yield: 8 servings (4 ounces steak plus ⅔ cup gravy)

Calories: 182 (32% fat); Total Fat: 6 gm; Cholesterol: 37 mg; Carbohydrate: 5 gm; Dietary Fiber: 1 gm; Protein: 25 gm; Sodium: 521 mg
Diabetic Exchanges: 1 vegetable, 3 lean meat

Preparation time: 10 minutes

Menu Idea: Serve with the Little Italy Tossed Salad (page 120) along with the Zucchini and Onions (page 154), both in this book.

Slow Roasted, Marinated London Broil

No need to marinate the meat prior to cooking, because in this super easy recipe the meat marinates as it cooks.

2 pounds flank steak	1 tablespoon minced garlic
1/2 cup sugar-free lemonade	1 teaspoon ground black pepper
2 tablespoons light soy sauce	1 teaspoon celery salt
1 green onion, chopped (with green top included)	

- Pound both sides of the steak to tenderize it.
- In a slow cooker put the steak, lemonade, soy sauce, onion, garlic, pepper, and celery salt.
- Cook on low for 8 to 9 hours or on high for 4 hours.
- Cut the flank steak into very thin slices on the diagonal against the grain of the meat.
- If desired, serve the cooked marinade on the side for dipping the meat, otherwise discard.

Yield: 8 (4-ounce) servings

Calories: 167 (35% fat); Total Fat: 6 gm; Cholesterol: 37 mg; Carbohydrate: 1 gm; Dietary Fiber: 0 gm; Protein: 25 gm; Sodium: 340 mg
Diabetic Exchanges: 3 lean meat

Preparation time: 10 minutes or less

Menu Idea: This versatile entrée tastes good with a wide range of home-style side dishes. Some of my favorite side dishes with this are Bacon Green Beans on page 102 in *Busy People's Slow Cooker Cookbook* and the Portobello Garlic Mushrooms (with only 1 tiny carb) on page 13 in *Busy People's Down-Home Cooking Without the Down-Home Fat.*

Slow Roasted Cornish Hens

These Cornish hens are as tender and melt-in-your-mouth-savory-delicious as any five-star restaurant serves. They are undeniably impressive for a special event.

1 teaspoon dried thyme	2 Cornish game hens
1 teaspoon dried basil	1 small onion, halved
1 teaspoon lemon-pepper	

- In a small bowl stir the thyme, basil, and lemon-pepper together until well mixed.

For each hen:
- Sprinkle ½ teaspoon of the seasoning mixture into the cavity.
- Put half of the onion into the cavity.
- Sprinkle 1 teaspoon of seasoning mixture on the outside.
- Wrap each hen securely in foil.
- Place the wrapped hens in a large slow cooker.
- Cook on high for 3 to 4 hours or on low for 8 to 9 hours.
- Very carefully open the foil so you don't get a steam burn.
- Let the hens sit a few minutes before serving. Remove the skin before eating.

Yield: 2 (1-hen) servings

Calories: 337 (27% fat); Total Fat: 10 gm; Cholesterol: 264 mg; Carbohydrate: 1 gm; Dietary Fiber: 0 gm; Protein: 58 gm; Sodium: 317 mg
Diabetic Exchanges: 8 lean meat

Preparation time: 10 minutes.

Menu Idea: From *Busy People's Down-Home Cooking Without the Down-Home Fat* serve homemade Mint Tea (with no carbs) on page 208 and the Tomato Zing Salad (with 6 carbs) on page 52. Add the Portobello Garlic Mushrooms (with only 1 carb) on page 13 of the same book.

Savory Seasoning Rub

The horseradish is my little secret ingredient that adds just the right amount of delicious excitement to keep my dining guests curious as to, "What's in this seasoning that tastes so good?"

1/2 teaspoon oregano	1/2 teaspoon onion powder
1/2 teaspoon dried thyme	1/2 teaspoon dried parsley
1/2 teaspoon horseradish	1/2 teaspoon garlic salt

- In a small Ziploc bag, put the oregano, thyme, horseradish, onion powder, parsley, and garlic salt. Seal the bag, shake, and rub the bag with your hands until the ingredients are well mixed.
- Use as a rub, about 1/2 teaspoon on every 4-ounce serving, before cooking your favorite meat or chicken. (The amount of seasoning you use will depend on how intense a flavor you like.)
- Keep refrigerated until ready to use.

Yield: 6 (1/2-teaspoon) servings

Calories: 2 (0% fat); Total Fat: 0 gm; Cholesterol: 0 mg; Carbohydrate: 0 gm;
Dietary Fiber: 0 gm; Protein: 0 gm; Sodium: 82 mg
Diabetic Exchanges: Free

Preparation time: 5 minutes or less

Menu Idea: This savory-seasoning blend is terrific on pork, chicken, and—my favorite of all—steak.

Speedy Sweets

Brown Sugar & Spice Sticks

These are best eaten hot from the oven, because they become drier as they sit. However, my girlfriend and I enjoyed them with hot tea as a snack the next day and they were still quite tasty. They are very flaky and crispy.

³/4 plus ¹/4 cup Splenda Granular, measures like sugar	1 teaspoon ground cloves
¹/4 cup brown sugar	¹/3 cup finely chopped walnuts
1 tablespoon plus 1 teaspoon ground cinnamon	1 (16-ounce) box phyllo dough (20 full sheets)

- Preheat the oven to 350 degrees.
- Spray two cookie sheets with nonfat cooking spray.
- In a bowl stir ¾ cup Splenda, the brown sugar, 1 tablespoon cinnamon, cloves, and walnuts together until well blended.
- Cut the phyllo sheets in half to fit a 13 x 9-inch rectangle.
- Layer 4 sheets on top of each other, spraying each layer with nonfat cooking spray.
- Sprinkle the entire top layer with ¼ cup of the nut mixture.
- Gently roll the dough into a tight roll.
- Spray the outside of the roll with nonfat cooking spray to help seal.
- Cut into 2-inch long sticks.
- Repeat the process with the remaining phyllo sheets and nut mixture.
- Place the sticks on the prepared baking sheet.
- Bake for 7 to 8 minutes or until crispy.
- Let cool before eating.

Yield: about 30 cookies

(Nutritional information per cookie)
Calories: 44 (22% fat); Total Fat: 1 gm; Cholesterol: 0 mg; Carbohydrate: 8 gm; Dietary Fiber: 0 gm; Protein: 1 gm; Sodium: 31 mg
Diabetic Exchanges: ½ starch

Preparation time: 20 minutes
Cooking time: 7 minutes
Total time: 27 minutes

Cream Cheese Bars

These taste like cheesecake filling between two flaky layers of pastry.

5	sheets phyllo dough, cut in half	1	plus ¼ cups Splenda Granular, measures like sugar
1	(8-ounce) package reduced-fat cream cheese	2	plus 1 egg whites
1	(8-ounce) package fat-free cream cheese	1	teaspoon vanilla extract
		¼	teaspoon lemon flavoring

- Preheat the oven to 375 degrees.
- Spray a 9 x 13-inch pan with cooking spray.
- Cut the phyllo dough sheets in half to fit into the prepared pan.
- Spray 5 half sheets of phyllo dough with cooking spray, and then stack the sheets on top of each other in the prepared pan. Bake for 7 minutes.
- With an electric mixer in a medium-size bowl, beat on medium speed the light cream cheese, fat-free cream cheese, 1 cup Splenda, 2 egg whites, vanilla extract, and lemon flavoring together until smooth and creamy.
- Spread the mixture on the baked phyllo.
- Spray the remaining 5 half sheets one at a time with nonfat cooking spray, and then stack the 5 sheets on top of each other over the cream mixture.
- Beat the remaining 1 egg white until frothy. Spread on top of the phyllo.
- Bake an additional 15 minutes.
- Let the phyllo cool and then cut into 24 bars.
- Sprinkle the top of the cut bars with the remaining ¼ cup Splenda. Do not sprinkle the Splenda on before cutting into bars, because the Splenda will make the top too sticky and difficult to cut.
- Cover and keep refrigerated until ready to eat.

Note: For added lemon flavor use lemon-flavored cooking spray instead of the plain cooking spray.

Yield: 24 bars

(Nutritional information per bar)
Calories: 71 (30% fat); Total Fat: 2 gm; Cholesterol: 8 mg; Carbohydrate: 8 gm;
Dietary Fiber: 0 gm; Protein: 3 gm; Sodium: 132 mg
Diabetic Exchanges: ½ starch, ½ lean meat

Preparation time: 8 minutes
Cooking time: 22 minutes
Total time: 30 minutes

Peach Crumble

This is a light version of Peach Crisp.

3 fresh peaches, cut into $^1/_4$-inch slices	2 tablespoons light butter
I tablespoon cornstarch	$^1/_4$ cup rolled oats
$^1/_2$ plus $^1/_2$ cup Splenda Granular, measures like sugar	2 tablespoons whole wheat flour
	$^1/_2$ teaspoon pumpkin pie spice

- Preheat the oven to 425 degrees.
- In a 9 x 9-inch, microwave-safe, glass dish that has been sprayed with nonfat cooking spray, gently toss the peaches with the cornstarch and $^1/_2$ cup Splenda.
- Cook in the microwave on high for 2 minutes, stirring after 1 minute.
- While the peaches are cooking in the microwave, in a medium-size mixing bowl cut the butter into the remaining $^1/_2$ cup Splenda, the oats, flour, and pumpkin pie spice until the mixture is crumbly.
- Sprinkle the crumb mixture over the cooked peaches.
- Place in the oven on the top shelf. Bake for 10 minutes.
- Best served hot.

Yield: 6 ($^1/_2$-cup) servings

Calories: 80 (24% fat); Total Fat: 2 gm; Cholesterol: 7 mg; Carbohydrate: 15 gm;
Dietary Fiber: 2 gm; Protein: 2 gm; Sodium: 24 mg
Diabetic Exchanges: $^1/_2$ starch, $^1/_2$ fruit, $^1/_2$ fat

Preparation time: 10 minutes
Cooking time: 15 minutes
Total time: 25 minutes

Maple Logs

The biggest problem with these tasty, crispy, yet chewy, dessert bars is not eating too many. These are especially irresistible fresh from the oven.

¹/₂ (16-ounce) package phyllo dough (10 sheets)	¹/₃ cup finely chopped walnuts, divided
¹/₄ cup brown sugar	2 tablespoons Splenda Granular, measures like sugar, divided
¹/₂ cup sugar-free maple syrup	

- Preheat the oven to 350 degrees.
- Spray cookie sheets with nonfat cooking spray.
- In a bowl stir the brown sugar and maple syrup together until well blended.
- Cut the phyllo stack in half to form a 14 x 9-inch rectangle.
- Layer 2 of the 20 sheets on top of each other without spraying with cooking spray.
- Spread 1 tablespoon of the maple mixture over the top layer of 2 sheets.
- Sprinkle ½ tablespoon of the walnuts over the top of the maple syrup.
- Gently roll up the dough into a tight roll, starting at the short edge. (Like a jelly roll.)
- Spray the outside of the roll with nonfat cooking spray to help seal.
- Sprinkle with 1 teaspoon Splenda.
- Cut into three 3-inch-long sticks and place the sticks on the prepared baking sheet.
- Repeat these steps until all the dough is used, 2 sheets at a time. (You should have 10 stacks of 2 sheets each.)
- Bake for 7 minutes or until crispy. Let cool before eating.

Yield: 30 cookies

(Nutritional information per cookie)
Calories: 42 (22% fat); Total Fat: 1 gm; Cholesterol: 0 mg; Carbohydrate: 8 gm; Dietary Fiber: 0 gm; Protein: 1 gm; Sodium: 38 mg
Diabetic Exchanges: ½ starch

Preparation time: 10 minutes or less
Cooking time: 7 minutes
Total time: 17 minutes or less

Cinnamon-Nut Horns

These are extremely light with an exceptionally thin, crisp outer layer.

3 egg whites	2 tablespoons ground cinnamon
1/4 teaspoon cream of tartar	1/2 cup finely chopped walnuts
1/2 cup Splenda Granular, measures like sugar	3 1/2 sheets phyllo dough*

- Preheat the oven to 350 degrees.
- Spray a cookie sheet with nonfat cooking spray.
- In medium-size glass bowl beat at high speed of an electric mixer the egg whites with the cream of tartar, gradually adding the Splenda 1 tablespoon at a time for about 4 minutes, or until stiff peaks form.
- Gently stir in the cinnamon and nuts.
- Cut the 3 phyllo dough sheets in half. Then cut all seven half sheets into 8 (3-inch) squares. You should have a total of 56 squares. This can easily be done with scissors or a very sharp knife on a cutting board.
- Lay 2 squares on top of each other, lightly spraying in between each layer with nonfat cooking spray.
- Place 1 heaping tablespoon of the egg mixture down the edge of one side of one stack of phyllo dough.
- Starting at the side where you put the egg mixture, gently roll the dough into a horn shape. This is easiest done by keeping the corner of the dough that is the closest to your left side tightly sealed, like the base of a horn, and leaving the large opening of the horn at the other end.
- Spray the outside of the cookies lightly with nonfat cooking spray.
- Place the cookies seam side down on the prepared cookie sheet.
- Bake for 5 minutes or until lightly golden brown on top rack in oven.

Note: One (16-ounce) box phyllo dough (in the freezer section with desserts) contains approximately 20 sheets of dough. Wrap the remaining sheets and refrigerate for later use.

Yield: 28 cookies

Preparation time: 25 minutes
Cooking time: 5 minutes
Total time: 30 minutes

Cinnamon-Walnut Mini Drops

These bite-size cookies are fun to pop in your mouth, kind of like candy. It helps curb your sweet tooth without blowing your diet. A bonus of these cookies is the aromatic aroma that, while baking, makes the entire home fragrant and cozy feeling. (Please note: These do not store well and are best eaten the same day.)

3	egg whites	2	tablespoons ground cinnamon
1/4	teaspoon cream of tartar	1/2	cup finely chopped walnuts
1	cup Splenda Granular, measures like sugar	3	cups unsweetened cereal flakes

- Preheat the oven to 350 degrees.
- Spray a cookie sheet with nonfat cooking spray.
- In a medium-size glass bowl beat at high speed of an electric mixer the egg whites with the cream of tartar, gradually adding the Splenda 1 tablespoon at a time for about 4 minutes or until stiff peaks form.
- Gently stir in the cinnamon, nuts, and cereal.
- Drop by rounded teaspoonfuls onto the prepared cookie sheet.
- Bake for 12 minutes or until cookies are lightly brown around the edges.

Yield: 60 bite-size cookies

(Nutritional information for 4 cookies)
Calories: 59 (39% fat); Total Fat: 3 gm; Cholesterol: 0 mg; Carbohydrate: 8 gm; Dietary Fiber: 1 gm; Protein: 2 gm; Sodium: 52 mg
Diabetic Exchanges: 1/2 starch, 1/2 fat

Preparation time: 18 minutes or less
Cooking time: 12 minutes
Total time: 30 minutes or less

Maple Cream Pastry

These pastry squares are so super flaky, light, and crisp that you feel like you're splurging.

1/2 (16-ounce) package phyllo dough sheets, cut in half lengthwise	3 tablespoons Splenda Granular, measures like sugar
4 ounces fat-free cream cheese, softened	1/2 teaspoon maple extract
1 tablespoon light butter, softened	3 tablespoons sugar-free maple syrup

- Preheat the oven to 350 degrees.
- Spray two cookie sheets with nonfat cooking spray.
- Spray the phyllo sheets individually, and stack 10 sheets on top of each other in each prepared pan. If the phyllo sheets rip, don't be concerned.
- Bake for 10 minutes or until light and crispy and golden brown.
- While the phyllo dough is baking, in a medium bowl with electric mixer beat together the cream cheese, butter, Splenda, and maple extract.
- Once phyllo sheets are done, spread maple cream mixture over one stack.
- Place the remaining stack on top of the cream mixture. Gently press the top stack of baked phyllo dough sheets into the cream mixture with your hands.
- Drizzle the maple syrup over the top layer of baked pastry and, with a very sharp knife, cut into 32 squares.
- Serve warm or chilled. Cover and keep refrigerated until ready to use if not eaten warm.

Yield: 32 servings

(Nutritional information for 1 square)
Calories: 29 (0% fat); Total Fat: 0 gm; Cholesterol: 1 mg; Carbohydrate: 5 gm; Dietary Fiber: 0 gm; Protein: 1 gm; Sodium: 51 mg
Diabetic Exchanges: 1/2 starch

Preparation time: 15 minutes or less
Cooking time: 10 minutes
Total time: 25 minutes or less

Busy People's Low-Carb Cookbook

Cinnamon Stick Cookies

These are best fresh from the oven because after a few hours they become dry due of their lack of fat and sugar. Nonetheless, my friend and I loved eating them even dry. Even dry they are crispy, light, flaky and taste great with coffee or tea.

1 cup Splenda Granular, measures like sugar	2 tablespoons ground cinnamon
2 tablespoons brown sugar	8 ounces phyllo dough (10 sheets), cut in half lengthwise

- Preheat the oven to 350 degrees.
- Spray two cookie sheets with nonfat cooking spray.
- In a bowl stir the Splenda, brown sugar, and cinnamon together until well blended.
- Layer 2 sheets phyllo dough on top of each other, spraying each layer with nonfat cooking spray.
- Sprinkle the top layer with the cinnamon mixture.
- Gently roll the dough tightly.
- Spray the outside of the roll with nonfat cooking spray to help seal.
- Cut into 6-inch long sticks. Repeat with the remaining 18 sheets.
- Bake for 7 minutes or until crispy.
- Let cool before eating.

Yield: 20 (1-cookie-stick) servings

Calories: 47 (0% fat); Total Fat: 0 gm; Cholesterol: 0 mg; Carbohydrate: 10 gm; Dietary Fiber: 0 gm; Protein: 1 gm; Sodium: 46 mg
Diabetic Exchanges: $\frac{1}{2}$ starch

Preparation time: 20 minutes
Cooking time: 7 minutes
Total time: 27 minutes

Chocolate Chip & Sour Cream Soft Cookies

These are one of the softest cookies ever, and that is pretty amazing based on its whole-wheat, low-fat, and low-sugar content. They even taste great after they have been frozen and thawed, too.

1 teaspoon baking soda	1¹/₄ cups whole wheat flour
1 cup fat-free sour cream	¹/₄ cup real semisweet mini
¹/₂ cup no-sugar-added applesauce	chocolate chips
1 cup Splenda Granular, measures like sugar	

- Preheat the oven to 375 degrees.
- Spray two large cookie sheets with nonfat cooking spray.
- In a medium-size mixing bowl stir together the baking soda, sour cream, applesauce, Splenda, and flour until well mixed. Dough will be slightly stiff.
- Drop by rounded teaspoonfuls onto the prepared cookie sheets. Because these cookies do not spread much, you can place 18 cookies on each large cookie sheet and bake both cookie sheets at the same time.
- Lightly sprinkle the top of each cookie with about ¹/₄ teaspoon chocolate chips, about 5 to 7 mini-chips per cookie.
- Bake for 5 to 7 minutes or until the bottoms are golden brown.

Yield: 36 cookies

(Nutritional information per cookie)
Calories: 34 (14% fat); Total Fat: 1 gm; Cholesterol: 1 mg; Carbohydrate: 6 gm;
Dietary Fiber: 1 gm; Protein: 1 gm; Sodium: 41 mg
Diabetic Exchanges: ¹/₂ starch

Preparation time: 10 minutes or less
Cooking time: 5 to 7 minutes
Total time: 17 minutes or less

Almond Drop Cookies

Almond lovers will appreciate these soft cookies with a light, crispy bottom.

$1/2$ teaspoon almond extract	$3/4$ cup Splenda Granular, measures like sugar
$1/2$ teaspoon baking soda	
$1/2$ cup fat-free sour cream	1 cup whole wheat flour
$1/4$ cup no-sugar-added applesauce	2 tablespoons finely chopped almonds, toasted

- Preheat the oven to 400 degrees.
- Spray two cookie sheets with nonfat cooking spray.
- In a medium-size mixing bowl stir together the almond extract, baking soda, sour cream, and applesauce until well blended.
- Stir in the Splenda, flour, and almonds until well mixed. Dough will be slightly stiff.
- Drop by rounded teaspoonfuls onto prepared cookie sheets.
- Bake for 5 minutes or until the bottoms are golden brown.

Yield: 30 cookies

(Nutritional information per cookie)
Calories: 24 (0% fat); Total Fat: 0 gm; Cholesterol: 1 mg; Carbohydrate: 5 gm; Dietary Fiber: 1 gm; Protein: 1 gm; Sodium: 25 mg
Diabetic Exchanges: $1/2$ starch

Preparation time: 5 minutes or less
Cooking time: 5 minutes
Total time: 10 minutes

Candied Watermelon

This is one of my all-time absolute most favorite desserts, and I cannot take one ounce of credit for it, because my assistant Karen Schwanbeck suggested the idea when we had some leftover watermelon from testing other recipes. This was simply a spur of the moment thought and the flavor is like eating candy. I love it! It tastes like sweet, cold, wet, tangy candy. It's the perfect answer to curb your sweet tooth without blowing your carbs or calories.

| 4 | cups chopped, seedless watermelon | 1 | (0.3-ounce) box sugar-free, strawberry-flavored gelatin mix (do not make as directed) |

- Cut the watermelon into bite-size pieces and put into a Ziploc bag.
- Sprinkle the watermelon with the gelatin and gently shake the bag until all of the watermelon is covered with the gelatin.
- Keep refrigerated until ready to eat.
- Serve chilled.

Yield: 6 (²/₃-cup) servings

(Nutritional information per serving)
Calories: 35 (0% fat); Total Fat: 0 gm; Cholesterol: 0 mg; Carbohydrate: 8 gm; Dietary Fiber: 0 gm; Protein: 1 gm; Sodium: 33 mg
Diabetic Exchanges: ½ fruit

Preparation time: 5 minutes or less

Tropical Watermelon

The blend of the Hawaiian Island's tropical flavors, including pineapple, coconut, and coconut cream, makes this an ideal dessert to serve at a Hawaiian-theme meal or party, especially if the weather is hot. For added pizzazz, I like to display the pretty colors of this simple but sweet dessert in a trifle bowl, because the height of the trifle bowl gives a special element to an otherwise boring dinner table or buffet.

4	cups cubed, seedless watermelon	2	tablespoons shredded coconut
2	tablespoons virgin piña colada drink mix (do not make as directed)		

- Place the watermelon in a pretty serving or trifle bowl.
- Drizzle the piña colada drink mix over the top of the watermelon pieces.
- Lightly sprinkle with the shredded coconut.
- Cover and keep chilled until ready to serve.

Yield: 6 (⅔-cup) servings

Calories: 45 (17% fat); Total Fat: 1 gm; Cholesterol: 0 mg; Carbohydrate: 10 gm; Dietary Fiber: 1 gm; Protein: 1 gm; Sodium: 6 mg
Diabetic Exchanges: ½ fruit

Preparation time: 10 minutes or less

Snow-Covered Watermelon

Super simple to make, this tasty favorite is requested often for summer gatherings.

6 cups cubed, seedless watermelon, chilled	1 teaspoon almond flavoring
6 individual packets Splenda	2 tablespoons shredded coconut
1 (8-ounce) fat-free dessert whipped topping	

- Put the melon in a 9 x 13-inch glass casserole dish.
- Gently toss the watermelon with the Splenda.
- Stir the dessert topping with the almond flavoring.
- Spread the topping on the watermelon.
- Sprinkle with the coconut.
- Cover and keep chilled until ready to eat.

Note: Honeydew and cantaloupe can be used as well.

Yield: 12 ($\frac{1}{2}$-cup) servings

Calories: 62 (0% fat); Total Fat: 0 gm; Cholesterol: 0 mg; Carbohydrate: 13 gm;
Dietary Fiber: 0 gm; Protein: 0 gm; Sodium: 14 mg
Diabetic Exchanges: $\frac{1}{2}$ fruit, $\frac{1}{2}$ other carbohydrate

Preparation time: 8 minutes

Watermelon Soft Sorbet

I feel like I am at an expensive restaurant splurging when eating this.

3	teaspoons lime juice	1/2	cup Splenda Granular, measures like sugar
6	cups firmly packed frozen cubed watermelon*	1	cup cold water

- In a blender put the lime juice, frozen watermelon, Splenda, and water.
- Cover and process on the highest speed for 1 to 2 minutes or until smooth.
- Serve in dessert cups immediately. Garnish each dessert cup with a sprig of fresh mint if desired.

Note: Cut the watermelon into pieces and freeze in Ziploc bags until ready to use. Frozen watermelon in and of itself is also a good healthy alternative to popsicles.

Yield: 5 (1/2-cup) servings

Calories: 65 (0% fat); Total Fat: 0 gm; Cholesterol: 0 mg; Carbohydrate: 16 gm; Dietary Fiber: 1 gm; Protein: 1 gm; Sodium: 2 mg
Diabetic Exchanges: 1 fruit

Preparation time: 5 minutes or less

Very Cherry Soft Sorbet

Very fruity and flavorful, this soft-served sorbet is one of the best I have ever eaten. It is that fantastic. It's smooth, creamy, and simply awesome for a light dessert on a hot day or evening.

2 cups frozen unsweetened tart cherries	1 cup cold water
3 cups ice cubes (about 21 ice cubes)	2 tablespoons Splenda Granular, measures like sugar
2 teaspoons sugar-free cherry drink mix (do not make as directed)	1/2 cup fat-free whipped dessert topping
	5 sprigs fresh mint (optional)

- Put the frozen cherries, ice cubes, cherry drink mix, water, Splenda, and dessert topping in a blender.
- Cover and process on high for 2 to 3 minutes or until smooth. You may have to turn the blender off occasionally and, with a long spoon, push the ice down until it is a smooth and creamy consistency.
- Spoon immediately into ten individual dessert cups. Garnish with a sprig of fresh mint if desired. Serve with a spoon. If you're serving this for an extra special dinner party, then serve in individual, tall, stemmed glasses for an extraordinary presentation.

Yield: 10 (1/2-cup) servings

Calories: 20 (0% fat); Total Fat: 0 gm; Cholesterol: 0 mg; Carbohydrate: 5 gm; Dietary Fiber: 0 gm; Protein: 0 gm; Sodium: 3 mg
Diabetic Exchanges: Free

Preparation time: 5 minutes or less

Citrus Berry Soft Sorbet

This wonderful, fruity, soft, creamy consistency with its slightly tangy flavor doesn't last long after preparing it, so make sure you have your dessert cups ready. It's perfect for something a little sweet after a meal.

3/4 cup fat-free frozen dessert whipped topping	1¼ cups frozen mixed berries (raspberries, blueberries, and blackberries mixed)
1 cup ice (about 7 ice cubes)	
1 cup sugar-free orange-flavored drink, chilled	2 tablespoons Splenda Granular, measures like sugar*

- Put the frozen dessert whipped topping, ice, orange drink, frozen berries, and Splenda in a blender.
- Turn the blender on its highest speed for about 2 minutes or until smooth. You may have to turn the blender off and on occasionally to press the frozen ingredients to the bottom.
- Spoon ½ cup of the mixture into small dessert cups. Serve immediately.

Note: Taste before serving and add 1 teaspoon more Splenda at a time if needed until desired sweetness is achieved. Because fruit has varying degrees of sweetness, the amount of sweetener needed may vary.

Yield: 4 (½-cup) servings

Calories: 52 (0% fat); Total Fat: 0 gm; Cholesterol: 0 mg; Carbohydrate: 11 gm; Dietary Fiber: 1 gm; Protein: 0 gm; Sodium: 8 mg
Diabetic Exchanges: 1 fruit

Preparation time: 3 minutes or less

Peach Soft Sorbet

I almost thought I had died and gone to heaven when I tasted this and realized how low-carb and low-calorie it is.

3 cups unsweetened frozen peach slices	**1 cup cold water**
¹/₃ cup Splenda Granular, measures like sugar	**1 tablespoon lime juice**
	Fresh mint sprigs (optional)

- In a blender put the frozen peaches, Splenda, water, and lime juice.
- Turn the blender to highest speed and process for about 3 minutes or until smooth.
- Spoon into dessert cups.
- Garnish with a fresh sprig of mint if desired.

Yield: 7 (½-cup) servings

Calories: 39 (0% fat); Total Fat: 0 gm; Cholesterol: 0 mg; Carbohydrate: 8 gm; Dietary Fiber: 2 gm; Protein: 1 gm; Sodium: 0 mg
Diabetic Exchanges: ½ fruit

Preparation time: 5 minutes or less

Easiest Apple Pie

To save oodles of carbs I use phyllo dough sheets (found in freezer section with dessert items). It also saves me a lot of time preparing piecrusts. This is one of the flakiest piecrusts I've ever eaten. I like it better than the traditional piecrust.

6	Granny Smith apples, peeled and sliced thinly*	$3/4$	teaspoon ground cinnamon
I	cup plus I tablespoon Splenda Granular, measures like sugar	$1/8$	teaspoon ground cloves
2	tablespoons cornstarch	I	(16-ounce) box phyllo dough sheets
		I	egg white, beaten

- Preheat the oven to 425 degrees.
- Place the apples in a microwave-safe bowl. Toss them gently with the 1 cup Splenda, cornstarch, cinnamon, and cloves.
- Cover the bowl and cook in a carousel microwave for 5 to 7 minutes, stirring every 2 minutes until the apples are tender and fully heated.
- While the apples are cooking, cut the phyllo dough in half to form a rectangle. Wrap one stack to keep from drying out, and save the other stack to use another time.
- Spray each sheet of phyllo dough with nonfat cooking spray. Stack 10 sheets (half of the stack) of the phyllo dough on top of each other to form the bottom of the piecrust. Place the sheets across the pie plate like tire spindles, crossing in the center. Allow the extra length to hang over the edge of the pie plate.
- Put the cooked apples into the pie plate.
- With the remaining 10 sheets of phyllo dough, make the top crust by doing the exact same thing you did with the bottom crust. The only difference is you aren't going to press the dough into the bottom of the plate.

- With sharp scissors, cut the phyllo dough hanging off the edge of the pie plate.
- If needed, spray in between the layers of phyllo dough sheets with nonfat cooking spray and tightly squeeze the phyllo dough sheets together to help seal the top and bottom layers of crust together.
- Brush the top of the piecrust with the beaten egg white.
- With a 1-inch piece of aluminum foil, cover the edge of the crust.
- Bake for 10 minutes.
- Remove the foil. Bake another 5 to 7 minutes or until the top is a light golden brown.
- Remove the pie from the oven, and sprinkle the remaining 1 tablespoon Splenda on top of the piecrust and cut into eight pieces.

Note: To save time slice the apples with your food processor.

Yield: 8 (1-piece) servings

Calories: 141 (5% fat); Total Fat: 1gm; Cholesterol: 0 mg; Carbohydrate: 32 gm; Dietary Fiber: 2 gm; Protein: 2 gm; Sodium: 99 mg
Diabetic Exchanges: 1 starch, 1 fruit

Preparation time: 10 minutes
Cooking time: 20 minutes
Total time: 30 minutes

Mini Strawberry Tarts

These are ideal for high tea. They are like mini strawberry glazed pies. They are so cute and so tasty, too.

2 cups plus 1 cup fresh strawberries, cleaned (about 1 pound)	1½ tablespoons cornstarch
½ cup Splenda Granular, measures like sugar	2 (2.1-ounce) boxes prebaked phyllo shells
	⅔ cup fat-free dessert whipped topping

- Purée in a blender on highest speed the 2 cups strawberries for about 30 seconds.
- Put the puréed strawberries in a nonstick saucepan with the Splenda and cornstarch. Cook over medium heat, stirring frequently until thick.
- Turn off the heat.
- While the sauce thickens, cut the remaining 1 cup strawberries into quarters vertically.
- Gently stir the quartered strawberries into the strawberry mixture, covering all the berries.
- Put 1 heaping teaspoon prepared berries into each phyllo shell.
- Top each mini pie with 1 teaspoon dessert topping.
- Cover and keep chilled until ready to eat.

Yield: 15 (2-tart) servings

Calories: 61 (36% fat); Total Fat: 2 gm; Cholesterol: 0 mg; Carbohydrate: 9 gm; Dietary Fiber: 1 gm; Protein: 1 gm; Sodium: 25 mg
Diabetic Exchanges: ½ starch, ½ fat

Preparation time: 15 minutes
Cooking time: 5 minutes
Total time: 20 minutes

Mini Blueberry-Lemon Tarts

These tiny tarts are superb for teas, light desserts, and bridal or baby showers when you want something a little extra special without investing a lot of time, money, or preparation.

4 ounces fat-free cream cheese	1/3 cup sugar-free blueberry glaze
1/4 teaspoon sugar-free, lemonade mix (do not make as directed)	1 (2.1 ounce) box mini phyllo shells (in pastry section of freezer section in store)
1 individual packet Splenda	
1 cup fresh blueberries	

- Stir the cream cheese, lemonade mix, and Splenda together until well blended.
- Put 1 teaspoon of the cream mixture into each mini phyllo shell.
- Gently stir the blueberries with the glaze. Top each tart with the glazed blueberries.
- Keep chilled until ready to serve.

Yield: 15 (1-tart) servings

Calories: 35 Total Fat: 1 gm (32% fat); Cholesterol: 1 mg; Carbohydrate: 4 gm; Dietary Fiber: 0 gm; Protein: 1 gm; Sodium: 49 mg
Diabetic Exchanges: 1/2 starch

Preparation time: 20 minutes or less

No-Bake Mini Strawberry Cream Tarts

You'll think you are cheating and eating lots of carbohydrates in this delightful dessert, but don't worry. You are not. It is also fancy and impressive, making it a good choice to serve at the end of a special meal.

8 ounces fat-free cream cheese, softened	2 tablespoons Splenda Granular, measures like sugar
8 individual packets Splenda	½ cup sugar-free strawberry glaze (I use Wicks)
1 teaspoon almond extract	
15 fresh medium-to-large strawberries, cleaned and stems removed	1 (2.1-ounce) box frozen phyllo shells

- In a small bowl mix together the cream cheese, individual packets Splenda, and almond extract until well blended.
- Gently toss the strawberries with the Splenda Granular and the strawberry glaze until well covered.
- Put ¾ tablespoon of the cream mixture into each phyllo shell.
- Top with 1 glaze-covered strawberry.
- Cover and keep refrigerated until ready to eat.

Yield: 15 (1-tart) servings

Calories: 46 (26% fat); Total Fat: 1 gm; Cholesterol: 3 mg; Carbohydrate: 5 gm; Dietary Fiber: 0 gm; Protein: 2 gm; Sodium: 86 mg
Diabetic Exchanges: ½ starch

⏱ **Preparation time:** 15 minutes or less

Peach Danish Tarts

These super flaky and crispy pastries are wonderfully delicious when they are first made. However, they cannot sit for more than an hour or the juice from the peaches makes the pastry crust soggy.

3 peaches, sliced thinly	6 sheets phyllo dough*, cut in thirds lengthwise
1 tablespoon cornstarch	
1/3 cup plus 3 tablespoons Splenda Granular, measures like sugar	

- Preheat the oven to 350 degrees.
- Spray two cookie sheets with nonfat cooking spray.
- In a medium-size mixing bowl gently toss the peach slices with the cornstarch and Splenda.
- Place 1 rounded tablespoonful peaches at the end of each phyllo strip.
- Spray the phyllo dough strip with nonfat cooking spray, and then lightly sprinkle with ½ teaspoon Splenda.
- Fold the dough strip with the peaches on it into a triangle shape, starting at peach end continuously folding to the other end.
- Spray the outside of the triangle-shape Danish tart with nonfat cooking spray.
- Sprinkle both sides of the triangle with ¼ teaspoon Splenda.
- Place on prepared cookie sheet. Repeat for the remaining strips.
- Bake the tarts for 10 minutes or until lightly brown and crispy.

Note: There are 20 sheets of phyllo dough per 16-ounce box. Store the remaining sheets in a sealed plastic bag.

Yield: 18 (1-tart) servings

Calories: 35 (0% fat); Total Fat: 0 gm; Cholesterol: 0 mg; Carbohydrate: 8 gm; Dietary Fiber: 0 gm; Protein: 1 gm; Sodium: 31 mg
Diabetic Exchanges: ½ starch

Preparation time: 20 minutes or less
Cooking time: 10 minutes
Total time: 30 minutes or less

Blueberry Blitz Tarts

I was so amazed at the flavor of these charming tarts. They're sweet, yet slightly tart from the fresh blueberries, with just the right amount of crispiness in the mini tart shells. Definitely a delightful dessert at our house.

1 (16-ounce) container fat-free sour cream	**1 pint fresh blueberries**
1 teaspoon sugar-free raspberry drink mix (do not make as directed)	**2 (2.1-ounce) boxes mini phyllo shells (found in the freezer section)**
	¼ cup finely chopped walnuts

- In a mixing bowl stir the sour cream with the raspberry drink mix until well blended.
- Gently stir in the blueberries.
- Put 1 tablespoon of the blueberry filling in each mini shell. Arrange the stuffed shells (also known as tarts) on a pretty serving tray.
- Sprinkle the top of the tarts lightly with finely chopped walnuts.
- Ready to eat as is, or cover and keep chilled until ready to eat.

Note: These are best eaten within a few hours of being made, because the tart shells will soften from the cream filling with time.

Yield: 15 (2-tart) servings

Calories: 96 (35% fat); Total Fat: 4 gm; Cholesterol: 5 mg; Carbohydrate: 13 gm; Dietary Fiber: 1 gm; Protein: 3 gm; Sodium: 47 mg
Diabetic Exchanges: 1 other carbohydrate, 1 fat

Preparation time: 15 minutes or less

Polka Dot Dessert

The fun name comes from its fun appearance. The blueberries and red raspberries look like polka dots all over the top.

24 reduced-fat, light, buttery-flavored crackers	3 ounces fresh raspberries (about 1/4 pint)
8 ounces fat-free dessert whipped topping	1/2 pint fresh blueberries
1/2 teaspoon sugar-free raspberry drink mix (do not make as directed)	

- Line the bottom of a 9 x 13-inch glass casserole with the crackers.
- Stir together whipped topping and raspberry drink mix until well blended.
- Spread over the crackers.
- Arrange the raspberries and blueberries on top and cut into twelve pieces.
- Eat as is, or keep refrigerated until ready to eat.

Note: Best eaten within a few hours.

Yield: 12 (1-piece) servings

Calories: 66 (12% fat); Total Fat: 1 gm; Cholesterol: 0 mg; Carbohydrate: 13 gm; Dietary Fiber: 1 gm; Protein: 1 gm; Sodium: 71 mg
Diabetic Exchanges: 1 other carbohydrate

Preparation time: 7 minutes or less

Kiwi Dessert

This is light, fruity, and has a slightly tart flavor.

8 ounces fat-free cream cheese	1 cup frozen strawberries, thawed
1/4 cup Splenda Granular, measures like sugar	1/2 cup sugar-free lemonade drink
1 teaspoon vanilla extract	1 tablespoon cornstarch
3 kiwis, peeled and sliced	

- Beat together the cream cheese, Splenda, and vanilla extract with an electric mixer until smooth and creamy.
- Spread the bottom of an 8 x 8-inch pan with the cream cheese mixture.
- Bring the lemonade and cornstarch to a boil in a medium-size saucepan over medium heat. Boil for 1 minute, stirring constantly until thick.
- Stir the strawberries and kiwi into the lemonade and cornstarch.
- Spread the kiwi and strawberries over the cream cheese. Cut into nine pieces.
- Refrigerate until ready to serve.

Note: For added flavor you can line the 8 x 8-inch pan with 1/2 cup graham cracker crumbs if desired.

Yield: 9 (1-piece) servings

(Nutritional information without graham cracker crumbs)
Calories: 56 (0% fat); Total Fat: 0 gm; Cholesterol: 4 mg; Carbohydrate: 9 gm; Dietary Fiber: 1 gm; Protein: 4 gm; Sodium: 126 mg
Diabetic Exchanges: 1/2 fruit, 1/2 very lean meat

Preparation time: 15 minutes

Fruity Almond Pastries

Super light, crispy, and flaky with a smooth and creamy filling, these pastries are best eaten the day they are made, because they lose their crispness. Believe me; they were eaten up very quickly at our home.

1 **(8-ounce) fat-free cream cheese**	1/4 **cup plus 2 tablespoons finely chopped walnuts**
1/4 **cup light whipped salad dressing**	1 **(16-ounce) box phyllo dough**
3/4 **cup Splenda Granular, measures like sugar**	1/4 **cup sugar-free apricot preserves, all chunks of fruit removed**
1 **teaspoon almond extract**	

- Preheat the oven to 400 degrees.
- Beat the cream cheese, salad dressing, Splenda, almond extract, and ¼ cup finely chopped walnuts together until light and fluffy.
- Cut 17 of the phyllo dough sheets into 3 long strips lengthwise about 3 x 13-inches in size.
- Put 1 teaspoon cream mixture on the corner of each strip and fold into a triangle. Spray the outside of the pastry with nonfat cooking spray to help the dough stick to itself to seal.
- Place on the prepared cookie sheet seam side down and bake for 7 minutes or until lightly golden brown on top and edges.
- Spread ¼ teaspoon preserves on the tops while the pastry is still warm. This will be a very thin glaze.
- Sprinkle the tops very lightly with the walnuts.

Note: Do not stack these until they have completely cooled.

Yield: 51 pastries (1 per serving)

Calories: 46 (21% fat); Total Fat: 1 gm; Cholesterol: 1 mg; Carbohydrate: 8 gm; Dietary Fiber: 0 gm; Protein: 1 gm; Sodium: 68 mg
Diabetic Exchanges: ½ starch

Preparation time: 20 minutes
Cooking time: 7 minutes
Total time: 27 minutes

Stuffed Strawberries

These elegant strawberries are just right for a little something sweet after a meal.

4 ounces fat-free cream cheese	1 pound strawberries (about
1/2 teaspoon vanilla extract	1/2 quart), cleaned
4 individual packets Splenda	

- In a medium bowl with an electric mixer beat the cream cheese, vanilla extract, and Splenda until smooth and creamy.
- Cut the bottom tip of the strawberries off, just enough so the berries can sit upright.
- Hollow the top of strawberries out with a sharp, small knife.
- Fill the center of each strawberry with about ¼ to ½ teaspoon cream filling, depending on the size of the berry.
- Cover and keep refrigerated until ready to eat.

Yield: 8 (2-ounce) servings

Calories: 36 (0% fat); Total Fat: 0 gm; Cholesterol: 2 mg; Carbohydrate: 6 gm; Dietary Fiber: 1 gm; Protein: 2 gm; Sodium: 71 mg
Diabetic Exchanges: ½ fruit

Preparation time: 15 minutes or less

Fruit Casseroles

I like serving this in a glass casserole dish, because the vibrant colors of this festive fruit salad radiate its sweet and juicy taste. This is especially affordable to prepare in the summer months when melons are in season.

2 pounds fresh strawberries, cleaned and quartered	I tablespoon sugar-free orange juice drink
I (3-pound) honeydew melon, cut into bite-size pieces*	I (0.9-ounce) box sugar-free vanilla instant pudding mix (do not make as directed)
I (3-pound) cantaloupe melon, cut into bite-size pieces*	I cup fat-free dessert whipped topping
I³/₄ cup fat-free, low-carb milk	

- Stir the fruits together and divide into two, 9 x 13-inch glass casseroles.
- In a medium-size mixing bowl, with electric mixer or whisk, mix together the milk, orange drink, and pudding for 2 minutes.
- With a spatula stir in the dessert whipped topping.
- Spread over both fruit casseroles.
- Cover and keep chilled until ready to eat.

Note: Cutting the melon into bite-size pieces is much faster; however, for a prettier presentation use a large melon baller.

Yield: 24 (½-cup) servings (two casseroles)

Calories: 53 (0% fat); Total Fat: 0 gm; Cholesterol: 0 mg; Carbohydrate: 12 gm; Dietary Fiber: 1 gm; Protein: 2 gm; Sodium: 75 mg
Diabetic Exchanges: 1 fruit

⊕ **Preparation time:** 30 minutes or less

Spiced Peaches with Whipped Topping

This dessert is exceptionally pretty when served in tall, stemmed glasses.

3 medium fresh peaches, cut into ¼-inch slices	**¼** teaspoon ground cloves
⅓ cup Splenda Granular, measures like sugar	**8** teaspoons fat-free dessert whipped topping
½ teaspoon ground cinnamon	

- In a medium-size, microwave-safe bowl gently toss the peaches with the Splenda, cinnamon, and cloves until the peaches are completely covered with seasonings and the ingredients are well mixed.
- Cover and cook in the microwave for 2 minutes. Stir. Continue cooking for 30-second intervals, stirring in between intervals until the peaches reach desired doneness. (For a total cooking time of about 4 minutes.)
- Put ⅔ cup cooked peaches into each dessert cup (4 dessert cups needed).
- Top each serving with 2 teaspoons dessert whipped topping.

Yield: 4 servings

Calories: 44 (0% fat); Total Fat: 0 gm; Cholesterol: 0 mg; Carbohydrate: 12 gm; Dietary Fiber: 2 gm; Protein: 1 gm; Sodium: 2 mg
Diabetic Exchanges: 1 fruit

Preparation time: 5 minutes
Cooking time: 4 minutes
Total time: 10 minutes

INDEX

About the Author

Entrepreneur of Cozy Homestead Publishing, Dawn Hall self-published her first cookbook in 1996 to raise money for her husband's brain cancer treatments, and since then she has sold over 750,000 copies (even though she didn't know how to type, use a computer, or anything about publishing). She shares her story in *Comfort Food for Your Soul* (2004/Harvest House Publishers).

Today, she is the award-winning author of the Busy People's cookbooks: *Busy People's Slow Cooker Cookbook, Busy People's Low-Fat Cookbook, Busy People's Down-Home Cooking Without the Down-Home Fat,* and *Busy People's Diabetic Cookbook.*

Dawn is a successful recovering compulsive overeater and food addict. She was born watching her weight. With more than ten years of experience as an accomplished aerobic instructor and facilitator for W.O.W. (Watching Our Weight), Dawn walks her talk, and she is living proof that you can have your cake and eat it too.

She strongly believes her talent for creating extremely low-fat, mouth-watering foods that are made quickly and effortlessly is a gift from God, and a portion of her profits from this book go to Solid Rock Ministries.

As a popular inspirational speaker and veteran talk show guest, Dawn has appeared on *The 700 Club,* CBN, *Woman to Woman, Good Morning A.M., Life Today with James Robison,* along with numerous other T.V. and radio programs nationwide.

You can visit her Web site at **www.DawnHallCookbooks.com.** To contact her, call, write, or fax:

Dawn Hall
5425 S. Fulton-Lucas Road
Swanton, OH 43558
(419) 826-2665 or fax (419) 825-2700
Dawn@DawnHallCookbooks.com